I0087178

From a Father's Heart

to His Children

Dr. Mark K. Mullaney

Dedication

As I see our culture drifting from order, my heart senses the urgency to speak hope, strength, and truth to my children, my children's children, and to their children. Losing my father when I was nineteen has burdened me to never forget that he spent much of his life protecting, empowering, and providing for me.

I dedicate this book to my beautiful wife Kim. Without her nothing in this book would have ever happened and I would not be who I am today. To my mother, who has forever stood by me with love and encouragement. To my gifted, blessed, and equipped children; Mark, Kevin, Matthew, Kristin, Kenneth and their remarkable mates; Laura, Meryl, Briana, and Nic. The joy and happiness I receive from each of you cannot be expressed in words.

I pray that my life has brought love, confidence, and affirmation to each of you. I look forward to watching as God continues to reveal Himself through your hearts.

COPYRIGHT © 2014 by Mark K. Mullaney
ALL RIGHTS RESERVED
ISBN: 978-0-578-15898-3

This book represents information obtained from authentic and highly regarded sources. Reprinted material is quoted and sources are indicated. A wide variety of references are listed. Every reasonable effort has been made to give reliable data and information, but the author and the publisher cannot assume responsibility for the validity of all materials or the consequences of their use.

Neither this book nor any part may be reproduced or transmitted in any form or by any means, electronic, or mechanical, including photocopying, microfilming, and recording, or by any information storage and retrieval system, without permission in writing from the author.

PRINTED IN THE UNITED STATES OF AMERICA

Scripture is taken from the English Standard Version unless otherwise noted.

Scripture taken from The Holy Bible, English Standard Version. Copyright © 2000; 2001 by Crossway Bibles, a division of Good News Publishers. Used by permission. All rights reserved.

Scripture taken from The Holy Bible, New International Version®, Copyright © 1973, 1978, 1984 by International Bible Society. Used by permission of Zondervan. All rights reserved.

New Revised Standard Bible, copyright 1989, Division of Christian Education of the National Council of the Churches of Christ in the United States of America. Used by permission. All rights reserved.

CONTACT INFORMATION
Dr. Mark K. Mullaney
drmarkmullaney@gmail.com
www.markmullaney.com

Contents

Forward

Family is the very fabric of society. The strength of any nation is found in the strength of its families. Sadly, that fabric is frayed and torn in many places today. Dr. Mark Mullaney gives excellent advice on how to strengthen families in his book, From a Father's Heart to His Children.

Dr. Mullaney speaks from experience. Although he has been a successful businessman and pastor, the health of his first family is his first priority. Mark and his wife, Kim, have always carved out quality time for their five children. From being a Boy Scout troop leader to years of experience teaching children in his church, Mark has shown his commitment to the next generation. Now he offers the cogent insights he has learned from their own family life.

The Bible says, "One generation shall praise thy works to another, and shall declare thy mighty acts" (Psalms 145:4 KJV). The measure of our true contribution is in how profoundly we are impacting the next generation for Jesus Christ. *From a Father's Heart to His Children* will help you do just that, and that is why I am happy to recommend this book to you, your children, and families everywhere.

David Shibley, Author
Founder, Global Advance

Preface

What a blessing and honor it is to pen the preface to this book. It has been my privilege to know Mark, Kim, and their children, Mark, Kevin, Matthew, Kristin, and Kenneth for twenty years. During this time I have also had the opportunity to serve them as their pastor. God has blessed Mark with a loving, faithful, and praying wife, Kim, who stands with him as his partner. Together they have led their children in the ways of the Lord.

It is my delight to watch Mark develop as a man of God, as a husband, and as a father. When Mark began a business from "scratch" several years ago, something got my attention: Mark declared that he shall seek first the Kingdom of God always before his business. Next to that commitment, Mark declared and exhibited his faithfulness to his local church. That is so refreshing in an era of "do-it-yourself, freelance" Christians who remain uncommitted to their local house of the Lord. Mark, together with his family, has been an example to believers through his involvement in church life including financial faithfulness. Thus, God has blessed him abundantly.

However, through the years of good success, Mark has continued to focus on the Kingdom and to father his family. Mark has continued to sow time into his children's lives. Many men who succeed in business do so at the expense of their spiritual life and their family life. Mark has been a man who has led his family in his passion and pursuit: God's Kingdom and righteousness!

As a result, Mark and Kim are blessed with a wonderful family. And, one of the rewards is this book.

Michael Hankins, Senior Pastor
Church in the City, metro Dallas

Introduction

"Don't you see that children are God's best gift? The fruit of the womb is His generous legacy? Like a warrior's fistful of arrows are the children of a vigorous youth. Oh, how blessed are you parents, with your quivers full of children". Psalm 127:3-5 MSG

In 1998, before I could graduate with my doctorate, I was tasked with the responsibility of choosing a topic, creating my thesis and then persuading a group to go along with my thinking. Writing in college or seminary often takes the form of persuasion—convincing others that you have an interesting, logical point of view on the subject you are defending. I actually had planned to write my thesis on "Raising Kids for Christ." After many failed attempts, I conceded! I was by no means on any level close to a professional like Dr. James Dobson, *Focus on the Family* and did not feel qualified to offer my opinions on the matter.

As I continued to pray, God opened my heart and narrowed my audience to my five children. It was such a relief. I would share my heart with my own children and if somebody else happened to glean some answers from it, then that would be a validating bonus.

Seventeen years after my first manuscript was completed and accepted (and I graduated), I discovered that my precepts and thoughts on parenting had endured the test of time. Looking back, my family and I enjoyed more good times than can be remembered. We also endured some very tragic events. Yet, we remain together as a family even though we presently live in four different states, in two different countries and cross the International Date Line. We not only survived my parenting precepts and choices but also thrived together as we learned how to be a family. My hope today is that the lessons I have learned as a father will bless others, regardless of gender, or if they find themselves raising children alone.

My audience has enlarged. Today, I present this book not only to my five children, their amazing spouses, and my precious grandchildren, but also to the many others who choose to read...*From a Father's Heart to His Children*.

Chapter 1

In the Beginning

God Knew You Before I Did

The second I laid eyes on my children, I knew they were mine. I instantly recognized each one of them as my own flesh and blood. We had an immediate spiritual connection and I was certain that even as newborn infants, they knew who I was as well. That type of connection caused my fatherly protective instincts to kick in and I couldn't help but critique the birthing room staff. Were they capable of providing adequate infant care for my child? They would have to prove themselves!

It's not that the hospital staff lacked experienced—they were more than qualified, but I had never really spent much time holding babies until my first one was born. Yet something inside me was raging with confidence, excitement, and an inner need to watch over my brood. God had supernaturally prepared me to hold my children more securely than even the professionally trained staff at the hospital.

In one split second, God gave me a heart to be their father—to love them, hold them, care for them, defend them, feed them, shelter them, protect them, and most importantly, to receive them as an extension of my life, giving them an identity, a divine connection on earth—my surname: Mullaney! I felt like William Wallace of Scotland—just try to hurt them or take them away from me. I'll crush you like a worm!

Their eyes looked like mine and their smiles were warm and true just like their mother's smile. With such amazement and profound humility, I was smitten with the realization that by God's design, the life inside me had joined with the life inside my wife, Kim, and over an eight-year period, our five little people were born. God's breath had given each of them a soul, a spirit, a body, and a life. How amazing! They would each have a unique calling, unique talents, and unique personalities. What a wonderful, precious, glorious, miraculous gift from God.

As I studied the Word of God, it became abundantly clear that I would only have these little blessings for a season. Each would grow, learn, and launch into their respective spheres of influence. So this was my hour, my allotted time to raise them to the best of my ability. Their callings were not in my hands, but in the hands of our Father God. He just entrusted me to love, accept, excite, rear, and discipline them.

True love wasn't always easy on their little backsides, but our children are intimately woven into God's plan. They have been so since creation. We must therefore take our responsibility as fathers seriously. Paying a small price for rebellion when our children are young can keep them from paying an even greater price when they are matured. Being a parent is not a popularity contest. But in some ways, as our kids grow, they are engaged in a beauty pageant, but not beauty as the world judges it. Instead, they are judged by the beauty of their character.

God has a divine plan and purpose for each of us. The Word of God reveals this, but when I first became a father, I couldn't help but wonder about the practical implications of such a daunting responsibility. How would I learn to coach them to go in the direction of the Lord? Yet, this was my responsibility. Would I accept this true calling from God?

This has been the greatest quest of my life and I accepted it with humility and appreciation. I accepted the fact that raising my children, and getting to spend time with them as their earthly father, was a gift from God. He had chosen and blessed me with this awesome responsibility and I was going to put my whole heart into it.

Even though my love for them grew with each passing day, I knew my time with them would be limited to seventeen or eighteen years. So I made a life plan to take advantage of the situation. While we were sharing love, respect, fun, hugs, smiles, practical jokes, and laughter, I was going to soak it all in, encouraging them to never stop. If an event, or a cause, or an activity was important to them, it was going to become important to me. And I'm so glad I did.

When speaking to the prophet Jeremiah (1:5), God was saying, "Yes Jeremiah! You do have the ability and authority to speak as a prophet on my behalf." God personally assigned him the task as prophet and empowered him, but Jeremiah wasn't exactly thrilled about his calling. God told the whining, complaining prophet to pipe down, grow up, and get busy doing what He had put him on earth to do.

The subtle implication is that God spends time with each of us even before we are born. Then when we are spiritually born again, He begins to reveal our calling and purpose. It is clear that this happened with Jeremiah. God spent time with him in heaven before he arrived in an earth suit (body). Since God is the same yesterday, today, and forever, we can learn about our own destiny by spending time with God. In fact, the Scriptures explicitly point us in this direction.

It may be news to you and it may seem strange, but the body that encompasses your spirit is just an earth suit. Your spirit has been alive since God created all of us and it will live into eternity as well. The greater question is, where? I like to dwell on the idea that my spirit man is as old as Moses, Adam, Paul, and even you. Genesis 1:26 says, "Let us make man in our image . . ." The earth has never been overpopulated because God knows exactly what He is doing.

We are not an accident. God created us for a specific purpose. It is our responsibility to meet with Him to discover our calling. When God was speaking with Jeremiah (1:5) He says, "Before I formed you in the womb I knew you . . ." This means we were in existence in heavenly or spiritual realms since the creation of mankind. This revelation has become one of the Bible's most amazing truths for me. Until I came to this understanding, I believed Kim and I were responsible for planning our children's births.

As parents, we are an integral part of pointing our children toward the path God has set for them. But ultimately, as our children grow into adults, they are responsible for meeting with God for further instruction. He did it this way so we would search for Him.

> "For you formed my inward parts; you knitted me together in my mother's womb. I praise you, for I am fearfully and wonderfully made. Wonderful are your works; my soul knows it very well. My frame was not hidden from you, when I was being made in secret, intricately woven in the depths of the earth. Your eyes saw my unformed substance; in your book were written, every one of them, the days that were formed for me, when as yet there was none of them." (Psalm 139:13-16)

By understanding that God took the time to create my children solely for His purpose, I became acutely aware of my calling as a father. This knowledge afforded me a strong sense of responsibility. I was the recipient of His children whom He already knew personally. He gave me the awesome responsibility of raising them. But was I able to accomplish this? Would my children trust, love, and want to emulate me? Could I provide the kind of parenting that would make my children go further than I had ever gone? By the grace of God, I stopped long enough to listen to Him and follow His direction.

I began to seek God on behalf of my kids. I would pray, "Lord, what is Your perfect will for my children? I need Your wisdom—not the world's wisdom, not my wisdom, but Your wisdom to raise these children." I distinctly heard God's voice on more than one occasion. While my children slept in their cribs, I heard Him say, "This one shall . . ."

This type of talk might sound frightening at first, but Isaiah had a sense of destiny, and God's calling on his life was evident from his birth. Interestingly enough, the Bible only mentions Isaiah's father, Amoz. His mother is never mentioned. I believe this is because children receive their identity from their father. God not only carved out a clear path for Isaiah and Jeremiah, He also did so with Noah, Moses, Jesus, Paul—everyone.

The most important decision for us all to make is to say "Yes Lord!" This is your challenge as well. All people have been called from the womb to fulfill a purpose in the Earth. All have a divine destiny. But not everyone says, "Yes Lord!"

The Lord Jesus Christ was called from the womb with a specific purpose for His life (Isaiah 7:14, 9:16 and 11:1-3). Clearly, God chose to present himself as a man so we could grasp His heart for us. Jesus was most certainly the Son of God, birthed as we are birthed and challenged as we too are challenged. The believer has also been called forth from the womb and destined for a particular task in life (Ephesians 1:4-5, Romans 8:28-29, Ephesians 3:1-10). Every servant of the Lord must determine with confidence that he or she has indeed heard the true call of the Lord from eternity past.

This truth helped facilitate my understanding of the responsibility of fatherhood. I came to grips with the reality that to raise my children without a spiritual influence could result in a delay for them. I could lead them down a strange path that could cost them years of unnecessary challenges and risk—much like the children of Israel who wandered in the wilderness for forty years, or I could lead them in the ways of the Lord.

In light of this new revelation, it became urgent for me to hear from God for each of my children because, raising them my way was completely out of the question. I wanted to do everything I could to raise my children God's way.

I cringe every time I hear Frank Sinatra, Michael Bublé or Landau Eugene Murphy, Jr. stand up and sing, "I did it my way." I actually like that song, I love the vocals, and I think artistically the song and the singers I mentioned are pretty amazing, but the message makes me cringe. It can throw hordes of innocent people, including the singers, off track. I don't want to do it my way; I want to do it His way!

God placed the desire in my heart to see His will, His plan, and His purpose develop in the lives of my children. I fully believe that both my will and the independent will of my children would pale in comparison to God's will. I love them too much to waste their time on anything other than God's plans. Besides, His plans will be glorious—meaning they will bring glory to God and fill my children with enriched lives.

I have been so blessed to hear the divine call for each of my children. When Mark Louis was young, I heard the word "prophet." With Kevin Paul, I heard the word "healer." For Matthew James, I heard the word "peacemaker." Over Kristin Rose, I heard the word "oracle" and for Kenneth Daniel I heard "wisdom." Although I would like to see these callings come to pass in my lifetime, it is not my responsibility to make them happen. I would never force what I believe I heard upon my children.

My peace comes when I remember that this is God's plan, not mine. I am responsible to do my part, but our Father God will also follow through with His part. He does—always. His Word says He is faithful to complete that which He began. He has sent prophetic words to my children at various times to speak to them what I heard in the quiet place with Him. I have watched their lives unfold and have seen small glimmers of light that would indicate little confirmations regarding these words in my heart. Yet, as I write this book, I must wait to see the results.

I was never exactly sure how we were going to get where God wanted us to go, but I have learned to trust in His provision and direction. As the Lord's plan for the Mullaney clan unfolded, He reinforced my lifelong commitment to be a father who is committed to His ways. By the grace of God, I was never alone. God was and is always going to be there for us and with us.

God Makes Provision

> "Therefore I tell you, do not be anxious about your life, what you will eat or what you will drink, nor about your body, what you will put on. Is not life more than food, and the body more than clothing?" (Matthew 6:25)

A born-again believer has the choice of trusting God for his or her needs. Because of my personality type, I have to work hard at trusting anyone other than myself. Shamefully, that includes trusting God for the outcome. I like to be in control of everything. This really is a weakness of mine and if I am not cognizant of my own weaknesses, they can negate my effort to live by faith. I have learned that when I let go and allow God to bless me His way, my real needs are met and I am a more thankful, happy person. His Word promises us more than we could ever accomplish on our own.

Jesus is the Alpha and the Omega. He does not live on our lineal timeline. He does not prophesy about the future, as we understand prophecy. Instead, He tells us the future because He has both seen and is in the future. Since He has seen the future, our faith is complete in everything He tells us in His word. He is the beginning and the end. He is our future, and He has already seen it. There is nothing left for Him to see. When we resolve this in our hearts, we begin to walk in greater assurance and peace about every tomorrow.

In Acts 28, Paul and his posse were on a ship sailing to Rome. As the ship was being torn apart in a massive storm, God spoke to Paul. He told Paul that if the captain did not release total control of the ship, then everyone would die. Fortunately, the captain believed Paul, set the sails to the wind, and cut the rope to the rudder, leaving the ship at the mercy of God. God ran the ship onto a sand bar right next to a populated island. Everyone lived! God's way is the only way that leads to life.

Allowing God to take the reins in our lives enables us to produce at much higher levels. His Holy Spirit equips us with the tenure to stand in the face of adversity and withstand attacks from the enemy. Our faith grows and we mature. His grace enables us to manage through challenges. This faith creates a divine connection with God that empowers us to follow His will instead of our own.

The pressure that a parent can feel to provide for their family is real. So when we learn to trust God with the outcome, His joy fills and strengthens us. It is our responsibility to do the work, but God's willingness to provide the increase is what matters. "For you will spread out to the right and to the left; your descendants will dispossess nations and settle in their desolate cities" (Isaiah 54:3 NIV). This is not a prophecy—this is a fact. So be it. Let me give you an illustration of living alone, without God.

Just like the infamous Bob Wiley, from the movie *What About Bob?,* you decide to take a vacation from your problems. You get to the airport, get your boarding pass, navigate your way through security, and get on the airplane. Since your buddy works for the airlines, he coded your ticket to receive a pilot's discount and they move you to first class. Ahhhh, this is a vacation! With every first class seat comes a nifty new airline ball cap and a complimentary pre-flight drink. So with all your bags stowed, the flight attendant makes her time honored announcement over the scratchy $50 dollar PA system.

"Ladies and gentlemen, the captain has turned on the fasten your seat belt sign . . . yada yada yada."

You've heard it all before. The huge jet roars down the runway and soars into the air. The wheels go up and it reaches 35,000 feet. After the plane levels out, you hear your name over the intercom.

"Mr. Smith, please make your way to the front of the cabin."

As you approach the galley, the senior flight attendant says, "Welcome aboard, captain."

You blush knowing that if she finds out the truth, you and your friend (the guy who enhanced your ticket) may be in for some trouble.

"The captain has asked you to join him in the cockpit."

You do your best to hide your excitement as you nervously enter the cockpit.

"Morning," says the captain, "have a seat."

As you slide into the co-pilot's chair and attach your safety harness, you catch a glimpse of the incredibly complicated dashboard (flight deck).

The captain hands you the controls. "Can you feel that?"

"Feel what?"

"Make a note, you've got 270 souls aboard!"

Your face flushes and you're filled with panic. What just happened? A moment ago you were relaxing in your first class passenger's seat and now you are strapped into the co-pilot's seat flying this enormous jet—and there are 270 lives in your hands.

The captain unbuckles his safety harness, stands up, and stretches out. "I gotta get some rack! See you on the ground." He is gone in the blink of an eye.

Now what? It's time to come clean.

The flight attendant enters the cockpit. "Good morning captain, can I get you anything?

"Get me something? How about a pilot?"

"Oh don't be silly captain, you look perfectly fine."

"Stop calling me captain. I just found this cap! I'm going to crash this plane, we're all going to die."

She just laughs and walks away.

On the overhead viewer, you see all the happy faces—your spouse, your children, your friends and everyone else who has entrusted their lives to the airlines.

Lies and deception can alter your course and adversely affect the lives of others. If you do not come clean about what you have done, everyone on that airplane, including yourself, will die.

God Help Me

Your fate, and the fate of so many, is in your hands, even today. Our words and actions affect everyone we are connected with as well as the extended families and friends connected to their lives, and so on.

If you have been faking your way through fatherhood, or worse, are so self-absorbed that you missed the mission God gave you to help your children find His calling on their lives, then it is time to make a change. Reach out to the real Captain and confess the error of your ways. Ask Him to take the control and to show you how to fly.

Parenting and raising children is not for wimps. It takes character, stability, trust, and love. Are you living sacrificially for your wife and children, showing them the ways of the kingdom? Or have you embraced the modern notion that we are supposed to be our children's best friend? You can't have it both ways.

I know it isn't easy. Parenting does not come with an instruction booklet. However, God will work beside you and in you if you ask Him. He will be your Captain, if you let Him.

God Will Never Abandon You

"The LORD your God goes with you; he will never leave you nor forsake you." (Deuteronomy 31:6 NIV)

As believers, we can experience times in our lives when we feel a bit like that person left alone to pilot the jet without any formal training or particular skill. For some reason, perhaps from lack of good training in our churches, we sometimes develop a belief that says God leaves us alone to fend for ourselves as unskilled, untrained, believers who are destined for destruction. This is a lie.

"No temptation has overtaken you that is not common to man. God is faithful, and he will not let you be tempted beyond your ability, but with the temptation he will also provide the way of escape, that you may be able to endure it." (1 Corinthians 10:13)

God will not give you more than you can handle. He will not walk away from you and leave you hopeless. God prepared you long before today, for today. He knew you and your children, even before He placed you in your mother's womb.

You look around the cockpit area and see a microphone. In a bit of a panic, you depress the button and request a flight attendant to come to the cabin. The door opens and in walks the captain.

"Good morning," he says, taking his seat in the captain's chair.

"Wha-wha-wha-where did you come from? Who are you? I-I-I thought I was alone."

He looks you in the eyes. "All you had to do was call me."

"The LORD himself goes before you and will be with you; he will never leave you nor forsake you. Do not be afraid; do not be discouraged." (Deuteronomy 31:8 NIV)

God will never leave you nor forsake you. He does not put you in a position to fail. That does not mean we won't try that on our own. Philippians 1:6 NIV says, "Being confident of this, that he who began a good work in you will carry it on to completion until the day of Christ Jesus."

One of the ways you can feel confident in your purpose is to get plugged into a Christ-centered local church, if you are not already. He has people just waiting there to pray with you, encourage you, and instruct you. He also has people there who need that type of support from you. The church—God's people—is His chosen means of exhibiting His power here on earth. Don't miss opportunities to grow as a parent by unplugging from church and "going it" alone.

Life Lessons

What would change in your parenting style if you believed that the Bible was the manual given to us by God Himself to help us navigate through all of life's challenges? Can you learn to believe that God has a training program picked out just for you and your children? Genesis 1:26 says; He created you in His image. Is it possible that He has put the ability in you to carry out His will?

> "Therefore, my dear friends, as you have always obeyed— not only in my presence, but now much more in my absence—continue to work out your salvation with fear and trembling, for it is God who works in you to will and to act in order to fulfill his good purpose." (Philippians 2:12-13 NIV)

Knowing that He is in charge of your life can bring peace, strength, determination, quality, wisdom, understanding, and hope. The entire list of what God desires to give you is really quite long and impossible to write in a book.

You can rejoice in all things when your heart has settled the issue of your will versus His will. The sooner the desire for His will over takes your heart, the sooner it will become a living, breathing part of your life and the sooner God will plug you into your personalized training program. Remember, God's training program only lasts as long as it takes you to learn. Therefore, if you seem to be going through similar situations season after season, you may need to ask the Lord, "Why? What is it that I keep missing and what is it that I need to learn?" No one can love you as much as God does.

Dr. David Shibley wrote this:

It is more important what God does in you than what He does through you, because the quality of what He does through you will be determined by the quality of what He does in you. God will allow things to happen to you so that things can happen in you so that things can happen through you.

> "No testing has overtaken you that is not common to everyone. God is faithful, and he will not let you be tested beyond your strength, but with the testing he will also provide the way out so that you may be able to endure it." (1 Corinthians 10:13 NRS)

In others words, as you seek God's will for your life as a parent and the will of God for your children, you will gain a new confidence in your parenting and greater trust for a favorable outcome for the paths your children choose.

Chapter 2
Growing Out of Total Dependency

The Pre-birth Experience

This chapter may seem a little out of place. Pre-birth should come before the physical birth, but you will see that the information I am about to share with you fits neatly right where it is currently placed.

My children will always be my children, and I will always be their father, even as they become adults. But there was a time in my children's lives when it would have been impossible for them to have any idea or understanding about life; where to live, what to eat and so on.

> "But we were gentle among you, like a nursing mother taking care of her own children. So, being affectionately desirous of you, we were ready to share with you not only the gospel of God but also our own selves, because you had become very dear to us." (1 Thessalonians 2:7-8)

At the very moment when my wife and I learned that God had blessed us with pregnancy, we immediately received the baby into our lives and knew that our family had been increased by at least one. Our unborn pre-birth children were already as dear to us as those running or crawling around. We claimed each of our children before they were physically born because we believed their spirits and the life God had given them were alive at conception. We thought of them as little human beings and not tissue. We were an excited couple waiting on our special guest to arrive, and we felt exactly the same as God blessed us with each of our five children.

During this pre-birth period, they did pretty much whatever they wanted, whenever they wanted. They slept, wiggled, hiccupped and stretched. When they wanted to kick, they kicked. They each developed their own schedule and arranged all their own activities. They didn't need anyone's permission, and they seemed remarkably independent. But all the while, their mother supported them 100% of the time. She supplied them with 100% of their daily needs—nutrients, water, oxygen, protection, love, affection, and shelter.

They did not require a lot of my personal attention yet. I rubbed their mother's tummy, sang and spoke to them anyway. I knew they could hear my deep voice and feel my touch. I also knew they could sense my love and affection. I wanted them to know my voice, my touch, my love, and my affection, even before their arrival.

Meanwhile, Kim and I designed, planned, and worked hard on a room just for the baby. We wanted to make sure when they arrived that they knew they were home and with the same family that anticipated their amazing arrival. With our first child Mark, came numerous revelations. He didn't arrive on the scheduled date the doctor had given us. Not only did he arrive later than expected, we also soon discovered that he was sometimes ungrateful, loud, self-centered and not always as happy to see us as we were to see him. LOL. That's an infant for you.

Reality set in pretty quickly. Like all infants, he expected us to feed him, burp him, change his diaper and stay on the pre-birth schedule, which he had deployed inside the womb. It was endearing and cute at first. But this kind of demand will take a toll on any adult. In my heart however, I knew with time, love and retraining, he would learn to appreciate what he had and that his demanding nature would settle down. It didn't really matter. He was our child. He was so innocent, so wonderful, so perfect, so extraordinary, and so fantastic, that nothing else mattered. Oh yes, he was very normal. As a parent we are tasked with the opportunity to see our precious children as unique and not challenging.

All newborns arrive pretty much as I have described: ready to eat, sleep, soil their diapers, and burp at a moment's notice. At first it seems as though they are in charge of everything. Infants have distinct needs and absolutely no understanding. We had to learn how to anticipate their needs and stay one step ahead. As their human connections and reasoning began to surface, we would need to grow as well. God enhanced us with greater tenderness, grace, patience, love and kindness to teach them new habits.

Now that You Have Arrived

I will use my son Mark as my example because; the first-born comes with so many surprises. By the time Mark was born, his mother had already completely spoiled him...so to speak. He showed up impatient about everything. When he wanted to eat, he would cry and make noise until someone fed him. He wasn't even very picky about who fed him; he just wanted to eat. There really wasn't much that could be done to settle him down until he got what he wanted. Even getting him to nap or sleep presented a challenge at times. We had to lovingly teach him when to sleep and when to be awake.

At first, he wanted to be awake while I was sleeping and asleep while I was awake. Certain toys appealed to him while others simply hit the floor. My challenge was to train him to understand that he was not in charge. I was the daddy; therefore, I was in charge. Initially, all children believe they are in charge. If we fail at properly taking the lead roll as parents, this self-absorbed mind-set that children are born with will become a recipe for disaster. For me to parent my children properly, I needed to recapture my throne without breaking their tender spirits.

It was challenging at times and I struggled, simply trying to understand his needs. I do not believe for one moment that he had a good handle on what he wanted or needed. In fact, he did not even have a clue about his options. He was a newborn and my job was to help him realize we were on the same team and we needed to work together. He had never been anywhere or seen anything. What did he know? He was just forming his opinions and planning his strategy to retain my place of authority. But I loved him too much to let him always have his way.

It may sound like I'm complaining, but I'm not. You have to understand my heart. I thoroughly enjoyed the challenge. I believe it has been, without a doubt, the most incredible blessing to be a dad. All of these daily events were an exciting part of God's master plan for us.

God graced my wife and me with the understanding that we would only get to experience this level of total dependency for a short season in our lives. We knew our son would grow out of this stage and that our relationship would mature and his needs would change. So, when he was first born, all we wanted to do was experience every moment with him. Our life and relationship unfolded like a journey. Each day brought something new, something exciting, and something different. It was a once in a lifetime experience that we were not going to miss.

I loved to look into his eyes and try to understand his thoughts. I wanted to provide an environment for him that would be pleasing and one he would remember. I especially wanted him to remember my presence. I hoped that by constantly directing him in a godly manner, he would grow in knowledge and understanding and that he would eventually flow in the personality and character God had placed in him. He would become an individual with his own perspective on life.

My children may have been God's gift, but they were my treasure. Around this same time, God began to show me how closely associated His Word is with the life of a child. With each of my children, as their lives began to unfold, it brought warmth and excitement to the Word of God for me.

"Truly, I say to you, unless you turn and become like children, you will never enter the kingdom of heaven. Whoever humbles himself like this child is the greatest in the kingdom of Heaven. Whoever receives one such child in my name receives me ." (Matthew 18:3-5)

As an infant, my son's needs were many times met before he asked or made the entire house aware of them. In fact, his mother or I would try to anticipate his needs even before they became a concern or demand. Initially, infants are motivated by feelings. They include pain, hunger, tiredness, fear, joy and so on. These feelings captivate of all their attention. Mark, like all of my children simply saw us as their source to meet these needs. Their physical hunger pangs prompted their vocal cords to sing a hallelujah chorus of "Feed me, someone, feed me."

God's Word spoke to me even in Mark's hunger.

"Therefore I tell you, do not be anxious about your life, what you will eat or what you will drink, nor about your body, what you will put on. Is not life more than food, and the body more than clothing? Look at the birds of the air: they neither sow nor reap nor gather into barns, and yet your heavenly Father feeds them. Are you not of more value than they?" (Matthew 6:25-26)

Do I trust God for all things? Or do I sometimes start crying out like my children?

The revelations I received from being with Mark were far reaching. He was so full of faith. When he woke in the mornings, it was apparent that he had not lain awake all night worrying about anything. He simply woke up looking for something to eat. He knew he would be fed. When I held him in my arms, he had no fear of falling. In fact, as he grew older, I was shocked at how he would leap into the air from the bed or couch knowing I would catch him, one more sign of his faith in me.

I believe God expects us as Christians to have this kind of faith in Him. He does not want us worrying about what we will eat or what we will wear. He wants our focus and our trust to be in Him. Furthermore, if the eyes of our faith are fixed on Him, we will walk in total peace knowing He is present with us.

During the early stages of childhood, God wants to fill us with confidence and assurance of who we are in Him. In turn, my children taught me many great truths from the Bible before they were even a year old. As they continued to grow, so did my understanding of my relationship with God.

The heart of God can be witnessed expressly in the lives of children. His spirit of love, trust, hope, joy, and faith are abundantly present in the warmth of each hug, smile, and kiss from a child.

Learning to Be a Real Dad

During a radio interview I heard Dr. James Dobson share some amazing truths, "Because I love you, I must teach you to obey me. That is the only way I can take care of you and protect you from things that might hurt you." I used slightly different words.

We always used the word "correction" rather than "punishment." Kim and I felt our children needed to make some corrections in their actions that they helped craft and understand. Punishment allows kids to harbor greater anger and their rebellion tends to increase with time. Correction yields positive long-term results. Punishment yields anger, bitterness, and resentment.

"Because I love you, I must teach you to obey me." This is such an incredibly true statement. However, before I had the opportunity to hear this quote by Dr. Dobson, the Holy Spirit highlighted the following scripture and challenged me personally:

> "Children, obey your parents in the Lord, for this is right. "Honor your father and mother" (this is the first commandment with a promise), "that it may go well with you and that you may live long in the land." Fathers, do not provoke your children to anger, but bring them up in the discipline and instruction of the Lord." (Ephesians 6:1-4)

I wanted my children to learn to obey me, but I knew I could not go about this in a military manner. "Children, ten-hut. Everyone stand at attention now! Close your mouth and listen to me because I am the ultimate authority, and if you do not, I will punish you." God didn't treat me in this manner. He has always shown me His abundant grace, mercy, and love. We must learn to treat our children in the same manner.

My heart's desire is to be obedient to God, always. I know how much He loves me. I want to show my love to Him in every area of my life, but especially through my obedience to His Word. God loves me so much that He gave His only begotten Son for my salvation (John 3:16), and being disobedient would mean hurting or disappointing Him. How can I intentionally hurt or disappoint someone who loves me and gives me as much as He does?

One challenge for me as a father has been to impart this kind of love into my children's hearts. I wanted to provide a godly, enriched adolescent period so the love of Jesus that is resident within them might flourish in such abundance that they would always think of God, Jesus, the Holy Spirit, and their family before acting in haste and ending up in trouble.

My constant prayer has been, "Dear Lord, please make my children love Jesus enough to understand that through willful disobedience they will have to bear the pain of knowing that they have hurt You." As their father, I know this is the measure that will keep the spirit of obedience in their hearts and give them a lifelong reverence and deep respect for authority.

When I read Dr. Dobson's wisdom mentioned earlier, it was a great confirmation because I had come to the same conclusion years earlier. I said something similar to my children: "I love you too much to let you grow up with this kind of attitude. I cannot allow you to slide by thinking that what you just did was alright."

It's Not Always Easy Being a Dad

I believe it is extremely important that my children have some idea of the depth of my love for them. If they do, then they will understand why I must teach them to obey me. Being the father of four boys, scouting provided a great opportunity to teach obedience. If I accepted the challenge, I would become a scoutmaster and have the opportunity to carve time from my busy schedule to spend one-on-one time with each of my sons at weekly meetings and monthly campouts. I worked differently with my daughter.

I taught the boys to stow their food at night so wild animals would not threaten them or others camping with them. However, one night at a very safe campground, the boys decided to leave food out in the open. My assistant scoutmaster and I secretly went to work, acting as if we were wild hogs. We tore through the mess kits, camping stoves, dirty dishes, and kitchen gear while making noises with tools that would disguise our voices and make us sound like wild hogs.

The boys screamed for help. Trying not to laugh, we finished our mission and then went to sleep. The next morning, they told us what happened.

"We can't cook our breakfast and we were almost killed last night by wild hogs!"

"Did you leave food out in the open?" I said.

"Yes scoutmaster."

"What did we teach you?"

"Not to leave food out in the open," they said.

"So whose fault is it?"

They learned the lesson in a very safe way. Thank God no wild animals actually appeared that night.

My daughter Kristin didn't need that kind of jolting to get her attention. She had a very thoughtful mind set. She didn't always agree or follow direction the first time, but she did learn from the instruction. With patience and some occasional nudging, she would accept the wisdom and rolled with it.

As a father, I created myriad circumstances so my children would come to a logical decision without me having to demand obedience. This is how God has interacted with me so many times in my life. God's perfect will for my children only occurs, as they are able to understand and accept His authority.

When we are relaxing together as father and child, I strive to make our time meaningful and fun. I want my sons and daughter to feel fully accepted when they are with me. I want them to know they do not have to perform or do something special to get near me. I will take them just the way they are.

When we are working together, I see the joy of the Lord in them. The Bible teaches us that this is where we get our strength. " . . . for the joy of the LORD is your strength" (Nehemiah 8:10).

I have always held my children in my arms with great joy. From the time when they were first introduced to the world, I have held them with abundant love and happiness. With a strong, steady hand I rocked them to sleep at night. I carried them with me wherever I went. And occasionally, I fed them and cleaned them. Some areas of child growth and development qualify for a mother's expertise, but I provided all I could. I read to them. I sang songs. This may sound all one-sided, as if they were the only ones getting anything out of this. Guess what? After a while, I couldn't tell whether it was more pleasurable for me or for them.

They blessed me so much by simply enjoying my closeness. Just their smiles would bring a rush of unexplainable emotion. Was this "love therapy" for them or for me? It became abundantly evident that this love relationship was a two-way street.

The more love I showed them, the more love they showed me. How could this be? They were just infants, children. What did they know about love? What did I know about love? I am convinced that we have been learning about the love between a father and his child since God put us together. I believe God allows us to experience these moments so we can individually understand the depth of His love for us. I can testify that my love for my children continues to grow and mature. I pray that their love for me does the same.

I pray that my children have many fond memories of the fun and excitement we shared together. However, this is not the complete picture. We have had some rough spots that needed to be smoothed out. Discipline was not easy on me, but I knew it was a crucial area of growth and development for long-term stability.

Sometimes, my kids were a complete and total mess. They were not only babies, learning to crawl and then walk; they were also people who began developing some sense of purpose, likes, and dislikes.

I learned early in my God-given father project that I would ruin my children if I demanded their future rather than assisting them in finding their unique purpose. How would it affect your relationship with your children if you helped them discover who they are rather than telling them who you want them to be? Only by the grace of God was I able to help my children realize their passions, rather than developing human clones.

Teaching and Correction vs. Punishment

By the time my children reached five or six years old, they had come from total dependency on their mother and me to partially independent little family warriors. With their ever-increasing need to explore and conquer, they moved courageously out into the streams of life.

We have to be proactive in our discipline process and we must have unity as parents. More challenging for me was to remain consistent. Life is busy and so often it is simpler to let certain things go. But when we remain consistent with the areas that need to be corrected in our children's lives, they tend to relate more clearly to right and wrong.

Mark's world was shaped by truth and playing baseball. Kevin found his groove by outsmarting everyone around him. Matthew became the friend to everyone. Kristin's love for music and flare defined her every moment. And Kenneth was the steady levelheaded one who watched and learned from everyone around him. If I told Kenneth not to touch a hot surface, he simply believed me and rarely needed to burn his hand to affirm my instruction. That wasn't always the case with his four older siblings.

In their very early years, all my children majored in finding the no's in life and limited the time they spent in the yes areas to a minimum. As a father, it amazed me how many opportunities I would have in a twenty-four hour period to approve or disapprove of what my children were doing. If I told them not to watch television, I would find them watching television. If I told them to clean their rooms, I found them outside playing, claiming to have cleaned their rooms by shoving all their clothes under the bed.

At times, they stood boldly in the face of a big paddle, defying its authority. And in one fell swoop, they remembered whose children they were, and after the sting faded, they would crawl back into my arms, which longed to hold them. This was hard but crucial to their safety and to their development as obedient and respectful children—those who would soon learn to follow God's laws, precepts, and voice for the same reasons.

A crucial note about disciplining your children is how and why correction is so important. For me, I felt it must always come from a heart of love for your children and never from an angry or frustrated disposition. The most critical thing to remember is that you should NEVER use your hand to discipline your child. NEVER hit your children with your hands. Hands are part of you and are meant for loving, caressing, caring, protecting, giving, and guiding your children as they learn to make decisions for themselves. You are their head coach and not their drill instructor. A good head coach will know how to bring the best out of their athletes. Drill instructors care not about your thinking or personality. They demand that you become as they instruct.

I also learned to use stern, loving discipline and reason to reach into the hearts of my children. They had to own what they did wrong, experience consequences, and choose to make appropriate corrections. I loved praising them for making right choices.

This approach of keeping them on the right track will cost you time and emotion. It is not the easy route for parents. But it is worth it in the end.

Correction should never be given out of anger. There is never a place or circumstance where anger is permissible when we are correcting our children. Correction should always be understood and seen by our children, spouse and others, as coming from a heart of love and concern for the welfare of our children as they learn to make right choices.

The actions of our children can cause anger in us. Cooling off and gaining a proper perspective is critical for a meaningful and proper response. Sending children to their rooms also gives them time to reflect on their actions. Once we know that we are calm, level headed and able to approach our children in love, we will be able to affect great change in the hearts of our children.

Occasionally correction must be immediate and urgent. If your child decides to run into a busy street or a shopping center parking lot you must act instantly. Obviously, this is childish folly because they certainly do not understand the danger they have created for themselves. This is the parent's responsibility.

To impress the urgency of the situation it will require a memorable jolt. Not mean, not angry, and not physical...just a good memorable jolt. When one of my children would take off on their own in any dangerous circumstance, and they usually do more than once, my correction would come with a swift, loud and shocking experience. KEVIN STOP!!! STOP!!! COME HERE TO ME RIGHT NOW!!! HURRY...COME HERE RIGHT NOW!!! I may have also lunged for him depending on the circumstances. Your child may even begin to cry from the jolt. That's actually a good sign that you made an impression upon them. This is not the time however, to beat them down with angry words of correction. This is the time to bend down, hug them in your arms and say, thank God you're ok, you could have been killed!!! Restore them to a safe place beside you.

Take a brief moment to explain the danger they were in and pray that they remember that moment the next time they react like that. I would follow up later that day with a sit down discussion to make certain they understood my response and my concern. More than anything, I needed to understand if they learned the lesson.

All parental correction must come from a heart of love and passion for the health and wellbeing of your child. As stated earlier, correction must never come from a heart of anger, frustration, or violence. It must be specific and appropriate for the situation you are dealing with. You must always discern between childish folly and rebellion.

Using the same corrective methods on childish folly as you do with rebellion, you may quite possibly crush your child's spirit. Their self-confidence will be challenged and they may become conflicted by their true inner passions. Your children could become disturbingly withdrawn. This is partially due to the fact that your child may conclude that their feelings and desires do not matter. Parents are the very people who should affirm their children while they mature. We should discover and celebrate individuality in each of our children. PS...none of my children are clones of me ...thank God!

Correction done properly will result in a lifetime of respect, love and confidence in each of your children. The reward will be children who respect our authority, and the authority God grants to others throughout their lives. Your children will be the true benefactors because they will in turn be loved and respected their entire lives. They will be the first in line for promotion while maintaining a spirit that desires to excel, learn, and accomplish their goals.

Focus on the Family has plenty of good material on the appropriate way to discipline your child. I suggest taking a look at it because often times, the way we were disciplined may not be exactly appropriate or in some cases, even illegal today.

Life Lessons

As newborn infants, our children are totally dependent upon us for their every need. As they grow, mature, and learn, they need to become more independent. This process will happen organically because of human nature. But the key to bringing peace into the home is in the hands of capable parents. Let me explain.

When infants recognize hunger or pain, they will cry, scream or both. It is a natural response to a negative feeling. When they act out in this manner, the natural response of the parent is to meet that need and bring them comfort and peace. I believe God set it up that way.

What happens if we as parents never change that modus operandi? What happens to a child that only gets what they want by crying and throwing a fit? Why do some children never change from this method of communicating? I believe it is because they have never been taught any alternative.

As mentioned earlier, I prefer the word correction because it is a positive solution to potential long-term challenges. If a child is still getting their way at the age of three and older using the crying card, then the parents have never retrained them to use a more amiable approach. At a very early age, parents need to teach their children that they will not get what they think they want by throwing a fit.

The best way to begin the process is to simply remain resolute and consistent with your response. Meaning, do not respond to childish demands no matter how they show up. Reward them only after you recognize their attitude has displayed a heart change. As a father, I found it easy to disconnect from the childish display of anger and fits. If there was no emergency, I only responded when their actions and hearts were not on the warpath. I attempted to anticipate their needs before they recognized them. Sort of "heading them off at the pass!"

By being proactive in this manner, my children would receive everything they needed without throwing a fit. Little by little, they connected the dots and realized that they did much better by having a right attitude associated with their desire. Be careful however, they will become incredible negotiators.

It is our responsibility as God's chosen parents to lead, guide and direct our kids in the ways and purposes of the Lord. He knew them before he formed them in their mother's womb and He has written all of their days before even one of them were born.

Parents are to be thankful in and for all things. Children truly are gifts from God. We can trust that He knows all things about our children and each of us. He will always lead and guide us in our journey and quest as parents if we ask Him. He never places us in circumstances for which He hasn't prepared us.

We will accomplish His purposes in our family by keeping our hope, trust and faith in God the Father, Jesus and the Holy Spirit.

Chapter 3
Living in a Shameless World

Breaking Free from Society's Trap

The social demands and pressure on children today are unprecedented in comparison to just twenty-five or thirty years ago. The demand on their time is incredible. The competition felt at schools, churches, and virtual communities is so much greater than any prior generation had to deal with.

As my children began entering school, I recognized that competition between peers and parents was going to become a challenge. Peer pressure is real and must be challenged in a positive, encouraging and respectful manner. It is very important that we strive to never make our children feel belittled over the demands of cultural pressure.

Like all children in this predicament, mine also felt social pressure to have certain types of backpacks, designer jeans, shirts, and electronic gadgets. These trendy trinkets are supposed to help kids feel like they fit in with the crowd. I believe that if we allow our children to wander down the path of cultural acceptance, more complex problems will present themselves as social indiscretions conflict with true family values. So rather than buying into peer or cultural pressure, I embraced the notion that my kids could set new trends. Being different and not weird yields individuality and inner strength.

By sporting cheaper tennis shoes, off brand blue jeans and the like, my kids were able to enjoy go-karts, mini-bikes, guitars, pianos, computers, and camping gear that most other kids did not have. The major benefit I recognized for my kids even to this day has been the discovery of personal likes and dislikes rather than embracing the norm and trying to be like everyone else. Always give your children an edge to make themselves independent. Who they are, is more important than who everyone else expects them to be. They will flourish as individuals with self-confidence rather than riding the emotional rollercoaster of fitting in with the crowd. Who really wants to be exactly like the crowd anyway?

Multi-million dollar corporations target children for their market share of everything from hamburgers and toys to blue jeans and tennis shoes. Marketing gurus have figured out how to transcend the age and communication barrier with clever commercials they run strategically during optimum viewing times for preschoolers through high schoolers.

Parents find themselves in the trap. Children are asking for video games and free goodies with burger meals that their parents didn't even know existed. The children are convinced everyone on the planet has one but them.

Years ago, a rather ugly configuration of a doll swept the nation to the point that parents were standing in unbelievably long lines for hours to purchase the last known supply of these dreadful dolls. Every year it's something new. Recently, kids are experiencing a rubber band bracelet craze. These little wristbands spring back into shape right after they are stretched. What is it that makes fad-oriented children's toys so appealing? In my opinion it's mainly two things, marketing and peer pressure. In fact, with time, most of these lose their appeal, go missing and are tossed in the waste bin.

Unfounded hype sells most toys. It is the power of suggestion through relentless target marketing and the cultural appeal from peers that elevates the need. This coupled with the fact that everyone known to man—including close friends—have already succumbed to the nonsense. At times it was very difficult for my wife and me to explain to our children why we were not going along with the fad. That being said, it is also import to maintain balance and flexibility. Never be so ridged that you appear to be breaking your own rules when the time comes to give-in to irrational purchases.

Many years ago I was traveling with a young family. At best, we had a 15-minute layover at an airport where our plane had a scheduled stop. As soon as our plane arrived at the gate, my friend's wife jumped from her seat, left the airplane, and literally ran down the terminal to purchase a fad item that was only available in this particular town. She already owned somewhere around fifty of these toys, but she was determined to own them all, or at least have a very respectable personal collection for her child. I'm not sure if these will make it to collector's item status, but time will tell.

Hollywood does not help. I do love a good movie, but because I have a trained eye, I recognize when movies reek of suggestive and subliminal advertising. At times, if feels like there is some kind of hidden agenda to shift the culture away from Christian ethic to a Christ-less society. I see this influence in practically every movie. The subtle use of certain products and the lifestyles depicted are portrayed as viable alternatives to good ethics and integrity.

For example, movies often show main characters smoking, which prompts kids to think, "She looks really cool. Maybe I'll look just as cool if I smoke." According to Legacy for Health, "425,000 young people start smoking every year; 187,000 start because of smoking in movies; 60,000 of those eventually die from it."[1]

Today, many movies and TV sitcoms cast at least one gay or lesbian character in a lead roll. Others are casting transgendered personalities in the same manner. Certainly, this is their prerogative. I respect everyone's choice and believe it is their right to determine how they want to live. However, I understand the power of media and influence. This liberal agenda will create the idea that LGBT (lesbian, gay, bisexual & transgender) lifestyles are normal. It begs the question:

"Is this an effort to recruit our children?"

We also see sex education programs at the elementary school level creating confusion in the hearts and minds of our children. At a very early age, educators are feeding our children a constant diet of liberal glossolalia aimed at undermining biblical truth. They fully intend to teach our children the idea that men do not have to be with women, men can be with men, women can be with women, and having your physical gender changed is on the table too. We already see full-on studies coming from our universities laying the foundation for a sexual revolution based on pseudoscience. Data that attempts to prove that gender is a decision and not merely confined to your birth sex. I find this vexing!

I see this as a major cultural shift that is gaining strength and unprecedented support aimed at nullifying biblical truth and God's design for men and women. Everyone, but especially our children are the targets of this liberal agenda. I believe the goal of this movement is to create confusion for our children and destabilize family foundations. This agenda is crafted to present an alter belief system whereby our children may choose which sex they want to be and or choose to be with as they mature.

It is not my intent to offend or disrespect those who have made an LGBT lifestyle choice. I am however, choosing to raise

---

[1] http://www.legacyforhealth.org/our-issues/smoking-in-movies/?o=3571#

my children with biblical traditional family values. Unequivocally, this nontraditional liberal agenda is not going to be embraced in my home. That too is my choice and it must be respected as well.

I cannot remember in recent times when a movie or television show was not promoting sexual promiscuity. Josh McDowell said the following in his book, The Dad Difference:

TV shows and movies tend to reflect the values of the times. And how those values have changed over the years! In the early sixties, the biggest problem the "Father Knows Best" family confronted was whether Kitten should get a paper route. Today, the typical plotline is whether Kitten should sleep with Tommy on the first date or wait till she "falls in love."[2]

I believe Hollywood is using movies to influence and shape our children into a non-God-fearing, desensitized, self-centered, and aimless generation—one that believes all forms of behavior is acceptable. You simply live your life the way you want to and we'll live the way we want as well. That makes life just peachy for everyone. No rules, no hate-mongers, no sin to worry about. Everything is simply wonderful. "If it feels good, do it."

I cannot blame all of these anomalies on television, video games, social media, or Hollywood. I only want to point out that each media has its own level of influence in shaping the thinking and understanding of how our society and children see themselves. This effect also shapes how they see their families, friends, those in authority, and influences their worldview.

I have recognized from my travels to third-world countries that children who do not have extreme levels of influence from television, video games, social media, and movies do not suffer from the same self-conscious and self-pride issues that children in the more technologically developed countries do. They do not

---

[2] McDowell, Josh & Wakefield, Dr. Norman, The Dad Difference, Here's Life Publishers, 1989.

seem to care about what they are wearing; their only real concern is that they have something to wear. They remain in total silence while they stand and listen to adults speak. They give their complete attention and show respect for authority. They do so without texting, giggling, grabbing, or throwing something at someone. While living in Mexico and traveling to India, I recognized traditional value systems in the children I met. They appeared to be very family oriented. They loved to ride their bikes, play kickball, and even sit with adults, learning from adult conversations. Conversely, in our busy American society parents are shuffling their kids off to the babysitter, day care center, sports teams, and children's ministries—just about anywhere that does not include spending time with parents. Don't be surprised if your children turn out exactly like the folks who take care of them most of the time. Parents who have no other choice will have to make a very concerted effort to reverse wrong actions and instill the right ones.

In my opinion, we have not necessarily raised a generation of children who are totally lacking respect for authority. Rather, we are raising a generation of children who believe they are equal in authority with adults. Therefore, they may not recognize the need to treat adults, who are responsible for their welfare, any differently than they do their peers.

Magazines at grocery store checkout lanes, billboards on thoroughfares, radio stations, cell phones, Facebook, and sports idols all vie for our children's attention. Children are constantly bombarded and exploited with all this hoopla by confusing their newly discovered and growing sexual desires and need to fit in. As a result, the average kid believes he has to be the best, look the best, or have the best. I love how Josh McDowell explains this challenge.

The world our children face is unstable, immoral, and void of spiritual strength. Our society has a tragically distorted concept of morality that leads the majority of our youth to serious confusion about their own sexual attitudes. If we as parents and church leaders don't provide clear, loving, and logical direction, our children will seek direction somewhere else. Ignoring the problem, pretending it doesn't exist, or hoping our kids will glide through unscathed doesn't work.[3]

Sin Does Not Exist

Our culture is crafting a way to deal with sin. It is positioning the cultural belief system to respond to sin as antiquated and hateful. One clear message I see coming from the media, Hollywood, major corporations, governments, and society in general is that by dismantling the concept of sin, we free the people of any responsibilities before God.

If the moral disciplines of the church are no longer acceptable in our culture and if the moral compass of the church is not allowed to voice its opinion in public forums, then eventually society will accept all life choices as viable options. Then in one regard, this widely accepted deception may shift society even further left of God's plan.

Sin has always existed and will always exist. For this reason Jesus came to free all from the bondage of sin. He came not to condemn us for our human nature but to reveal the truth of His love and passion for man. Sin therefore is the daily evidence that we need help. Only the Lord can help us.

"The Spirit of the Sovereign Lord is on
me, because the Lord has anointed me to proclaim good
news to the poor. He has sent me to bind up the
brokenhearted, to proclaim freedom for the captives and
release from darkness for the prisoners." (Isaiah 61:1)

What captives need to be freed? Release whom from what darkness? Which prisoner is Isaiah speaking of? Clearly, Isaiah is

---

[3] McDowell, Josh & Wakefield, Dr. Norman, The Dad Difference, Here's Life Publishers, 1989.

revealing to each of us how God sees sin. Sin is anything that is opposite of Gods truth. Sin is a lie and when we choose to believe the lie, we place ourselves in bondage to the lie and are thereby held in captivity.

We have an advocate with God. His name is Jesus. He stands in the gap for us and through Him, we are no longer bound by the bondage of sin. Rather, we are forgiven and once we are freed by the Blood of Christ, we are empowered to share this message of freedom and salvation. In fact, that is the message and the great news for all. Unfortunately, this message goes largely unheard and is rejected while certain sins become largely encouraged and socially acceptable.

If the lie that sin does not exist can penetrate the hearts of mankind around the world, then it is conceivable that the church as we know it today could be within one generation from extinction or basically considered impractical for younger generations. I say this because even today large denominations are divided on foundational moral issues like abortion, LGBT leadership, and sexual promiscuity. Jesus says; "If a house is divided against itself, that house cannot stand. (Mark 3:25).

Of course, I believe the church is the main tool God established to carry His message of love, redemption, and salvation to the world. The humanist's world's view is doing its utmost to present the church as antiquated, hateful, and even hurtful for society at large.

I see some churches publically embracing humanism in a botched effort to remain culturally relevant. But the question is, to whom are they trying to show such relevancy—man or God? Just like parents, the church must understand its boundaries and thrive within that playing field. Yes, I agree we must learn and adapt to many changing situations. However, some things do not change and cannot be crossed, especially by the church. I'm talking about things like moral boundaries, murder, theft, lying, and cheating . . .

I could go on and on, but I'm sure you get the point. "Jesus Christ is the same yesterday and today and forever" (Hebrews 13:8).

Many churches have chosen cultural relevance over biblical truth. The word of God cannot be changed to fit personal lifestyles. A few examples I've recognized is a church in Dallas, Texas that primarily serves the gay, lesbian, bisexual, and transgendered community. A recent news story explained how a church just reinstated a Methodist minister after being fired for performing a "same-sex" marriage. I read about another main denomination embracing gay bishops and leadership. If this is required of the church so that we can maintain our relevancy in our current culture, our true message will seem conflicted. We will have to cherry-pick the scriptures that paint the picture we are creating. I'm not ok any of this nonsense.

I am disappointed at how the basic beliefs of the church can become diluted to the point that contradicting worldviews are embraced. The church at large is ill prepared to deal with these types of life choices. God loves all people regardless of their transgression. But God's Word does not change. He is the same yesterday, today and forever.

> "For the time is coming when people will not endure sound teaching, but having itching ears they will accumulate for themselves teachers to suit their own passions, and will turn away from listening to the truth and wander off into myths." (2 Timothy 4:3-4)

While returning from the Dominican Republic, where I had been given the opportunity to preach at a nationwide conference for pastors, I was challenged to answer a question that seemed basic and simple at first. On one segment of my return trip from Miami, Florida to Dallas, Texas, I sat next to a woman who was obviously disturbed about something. She recognized the Star of David on my signet ring and my "W.W.J.D." (What Would Jesus Do?) cloth bracelet.

"Are you a religious man?" she asked.

"No." I believe the Holy Spirit had prepared me for this moment.

> "And when they bring you to trial and deliver you over, do not be anxious beforehand what you are to say, but say whatever is given you in that hour, for it is not you who speak, but the Holy Spirit." (Mark 13:11)

I spent the next hour discussing the difference between a relationship with our Lord and Savior, Jesus Christ, and the hurdles of the doctrine of man and the church. I shared with this dear woman the simplicity of the gospel of Jesus Christ. She argued that I was simply sharing my interpretation.

I opened three versions of the Bible on my laptop computer: the New International Version, the New Revised Standard Version, and the King James Version. I did this because of her first argument. I let her read John 3:16 from each translation and asked for her interpretation.

> "For God so loved the world that he gave his one and only Son, that whoever believes in him shall not perish but have eternal life." (John 3:16 NIV)

> "For God so loved the world that he gave his only Son, so that everyone who believes in him may not perish but may have eternal life." (John 3:16 NRSV)

> "For God so loved the world, that he gave his only begotten Son, that whosoever believeth in him should not perish, but have everlasting life." (John 3:16 KJV)

She concluded that God loves the world so much that He sent His one and only Son, Jesus Christ, to redeem us from our sins and if we believe in Him we can have eternal life with Him in heaven. I asked her if she believed this, and she quietly turned her head.

52

The pivotal point in this discussion became the word "sin." This dear woman's greatest concern during our discussion was the fact that someone was keeping track of right and wrong and that wrong actions are called sin. That made her very uncomfortable. She told me she had a problem with the word "sin" and asked me if we could call it something else.

The mentality we have propagated in our world and with our children today is to call sin or any other transgression by a different name. In doing so, transgressions will seem less disturbing to the majority of people and therefore society will accept these improper practices, attitudes, and lifestyles more readily. Some quick examples that come to mind where names are changed to confuse the masses are; abortion instead of murder, gay instead of homosexual, credit instead of debt, damage control instead of dealing with the truth, and so on.

I feel such a burden as a father to teach my children the difference between right and wrong. But far beyond my ability to teach them is my trust in Jesus Christ our Lord to speak to each of them and give them the personal conviction necessary to always seek God's path of righteousness.

> "My son, if sinners entice you, do not consent . . . my son, do not walk in the way with them; hold back your foot from their paths." (Proverbs 1:10, 15)

The truth about sin is plainly outlined in the Bible, and the Bible is the true Word of God. Sin does exist. If you give yourself over to sin, it will destroy you from the inside out. Sin has existed since Adam and Eve broke their relationship with and trust in God. God's inspired Word is the ultimate truth and authority here on earth and in the entire universe. It will always exist until our Lord Jesus comes again and takes His people home. "For all have sinned, and come short of the glory of God." (Romans 3:23 KJV).

The word "all" means everyone...me included.

Once you commit yourself to Jesus, He breaks the power of sin in your life, and through Him, your sin has been forgiven. If you turn toward the world for understanding about what to do with your sin, it will destroy you.

Dr. David Shibley makes a profound statement regarding the influence of sin:

"You live in a time when you will have ample opportunities to compromise morally. Make a choice now against secret sins of the flesh. Remember, there is no such thing as a victim-less sin. Even so-called private sins are victimizing because they limit your potential and grieve the Holy Spirit".[4]

The Bible puts it this way:

"I appeal to you therefore, brothers, by the mercies of God, to present your bodies as a living sacrifice, holy and acceptable to God, which is your spiritual worship. Do not be conformed to this world, but be transformed by the renewal of your mind, that by testing you may discern what is the will of God, what is good and acceptable and perfect." (Romans 12:1-2)

Life Lessons

As I see it, we all have choices. There is no advantage to hiding or acting as though these massive cultural shifts are not happening. As a father I did my very best to shield my children for as long as possible, from some of the harder life challenges they would ultimately have to face. That being said, I did this so that at the proper time of maturity I could explain with much detail, love and sometimes regret, the nature of our culture and the situations they would ultimately face and be challenged with.

I decided that public high school would be a good time for my children to experience a full-on dose of reality. It was important that I still had a firm leadership roll in my children's lives as they faced semi-adult situations. In the high school years, my children had already earned a great deal of my respect from I

---

[4] Shibley, David, From a Father's Heart to a Son, New Leaf Press, 1995.

trusted many of their personal decisions. At the high school age I would still be a viable part of their final decisions and could guide them in making proper choices.

College age is not the time to roll your kids out the door so they can finally make personal decision on their own. They must actually have already been fairly independent by this age. Without some "testing the waters" years during high school, the primary launching during college or career is extremely challenging and dangerous. Launching too soon or too late is like throwing your children into a tank filled with sharks and hoping they've learned how to swim really fast. Forcing parental control at this age can result in a serious season of rebellion. Your children choosing to make right choices at this age is from a heart of love, trust, and respect...not fear. Decisions that result out of fear cultivate anger, bitterness, resentment and rebellion.

It is human nature, extremely healthy, and very important that our children gain independence and progressive control over their own lives as they mature. Each season of their lives should build their confidence in making personal choices. If they understand that all decisions come with consequences, they will learn to make choices that afford the results they are looking for. Obedience cannot be forced on a human being especially an adult.

So I believe as a father, we need to work closely with our children as they mature, always giving them choices rather than ultimatums. Practicing a soft launch in every season of discerned maturity gives both you and your child confidence for the day when all their decisions become their personal choice. The high school years are so very important because our personal influence over some of their choices should still be intact. At some point we must trust the upbringing we sowed into their lives. One day, the only influence we have will be to simply be available should they decide to call for advice.

God's word promises us in Proverbs 22:6 that if we train up our children in the way they should go, when they are older, they will not depart from it. I'm hanging my hat on that promise. Face it, what else can we do?

Chapter 4
Drawing Close to My Children

Make Time for Family

Fortunately, I grew up in a reasonably functional and loving family. I was raised around adults, extended family and had both parents influencing my life until the early death of my father. While my father was alive, I enjoyed a wonderful father-son, mother-son relationship with each of them. My family upbringing included stability, firmness and great love. I cannot ever remember a day that I did not feel loved by my parents. Maybe I didn't always realize it at the time, but today I most certainly do. The bible promises many things. One of my favorites is:

> "God will turn the hearts of fathers to their children and the hearts of children to their fathers" (Malachi 4:6)

Ever since I can remember, I have made it a point to have time with my family. Each of my precious children is familiar with the term "family night"—special times we set aside to create cherished moments and conversations that we will always remember. This season (the years my children are with me) will only come once, so I want to take full advantage of it.

We usually spent Friday night together. We may start with a favorite restaurant or just cook hotdogs at home. After that, we might compete against one another in putt-putt golf, or veg in front of a family movie at home, or play dominos, or have an intentional discussion. Our main goal is to spend time doing something together as a family, enjoying one another.

I have such a fond memory of a simple family outing years ago. All seven of us were sandwiched into my extended cab pickup truck (don't try this today!). My son Matthew, eleven, was looking at the scenery outside the truck and noticed a particularly ugly vehicle.

"Man, that shore is an ugly truck, ain't it?" he said.

I looked at my wife. "Sweetheart, you sure can tell we are raising our children in East Texas."

Before she could comment, my son Kevin, twelve, jumped into the conversation. "That's what I was fixin' to say."

I looked at my wife and grinned. "Need I say more?"

We weren't out and about on family night simply because we were bored. On the contrary, we made a concerted effort to designate this time as a high priority because there was always something or someone else in the schedule that wanted our time.

Simple little moments like these build family values and lifelong character. I can't tell you how many times we shared this little story about the "ugly truck" with each other and we have enjoyed it each time. I believe that creating fond memories as well as doing our best to be examples for our children helps create a firm foundation for the development of children into healthy, productive adults.

Isaiah 40:31 says, "They who wait for the LORD shall renew their strength . . ." The optimum word is "wait." The original Hebrew word is qavah (kaw-vaw). The prime root of this word means "bind together" or "become one." Interestingly enough, the word "bind" has many meanings as well, one being; "as one." In context, Isaiah is speaking about becoming one with the Lord.

They who "become one" with the Lord shall renew their strength. This is done by being patient and waiting on the Lord. The Hebrew word qavah is used forty-nine out of the ninety times the word "wait" is used in the Old Testament (KJV). Interestingly enough, this Hebrew word is an action. So it is not just sitting on a couch drinking a cup of coffee.

I am convinced that God wants families to move forward together as well as with Him so He can bring us together to become one in the Spirit. We are supposed to carry on the best we know how with the knowledge base we have at that time. In doing so, God will supernaturally give us wisdom, and place key people and tools in our lives to help us move forward.

A Special Bond

I believe God has placed a father's heart in every man. Though some hearts are wounded and deeply hidden in personal insecurities, I believe God gave men His heart even before He placed them in their mother's womb. You must remain selfless with your children so that this father's heart of love, compassion, strength, and hope can guide their tender and impressionable lives. It is only through your choice to remain unselfish and consistent that your eyes can be opened to see the true love your children have for you. Selflessness is the key to unlocking the true relationships God has ordained for man with his wife and children.

I can honestly say that most of my encounters as a father have been such a blessing and so enriching that I cannot imagine having missed any part of what we have done as a family.

Before I was married to my wife, Kim, she would talk about her desire to have a large family. In fact, the first time we met, she explained to me that whomever she married would have to be willing to have five children. I mentioned that my number was three. For someone who had not been prepared with a father's heart, even three would be a rather big order. She was probably just testing the water to see if I was a possible candidate. Since I did not even flinch, she was impressed.

Years later, I put my foot in my mouth while sitting next to Kim following the birth of number five, Kenneth. I looked into her eyes just fifteen minutes after giving birth and said, "Are you ready to start on my three?" Oops! We never really discussed that option realistically again. But my heart was so full of love for my children that I couldn't figure out why we should stop at five.

As each of my children reached the tender age of nine, I took them on a special trip. This was a getaway just for the two of us. We could go just about anywhere within reason and spend three days getting to enjoy each other without the distractions of everyday life. I wanted to build a memory that would stick in the hearts of my children for the rest of their lives.

From my perspective, I wanted time with my sons and daughter to discover their likes and dislikes, and to watch them think, play, and interact. I wanted to listen to them without any pressing distractions. I wanted them to have the opportunity to be themselves and to see old Dad really enjoying himself as a person. What a glorious time God has given me with each child. I am so thankful that we took these trips. I was the real winner.

Mark Louis Mullaney

When my son Mark turned nine, we planned a trip from our home in Dallas, out to the West Texas town of El Paso, to play golf, visit some old sites where I romped as a child, and attend his cousin's wedding. A huge part of the fun was sitting down to plan the trip. When we talked about how we would get all the way to El Paso, the "airplane" word came up, and the smile on his precious face stretched from ear to ear.

As he boarded his first airplane and buckled his seatbelt, I realized how blessed I was to have the opportunity to share in this moment. I watched as his eyes got big when the engines roared. On the day we flew off into the wild blue yonder, his world changed.

"I can't get up," he said. "The engine is going so fast my butt is stuck in the seat."

I just laughed and laughed.

As the wheels left the ground, everybody could hear Mark above the roar of the engine.

"I am flying, I am flying, I fly . . . Dr. Marvin, I fly!"

I wasn't entirely certain if family night had actually helped galvanize our family together until he busted out with that unforgettable shout. If you keep up with Bill Murray movies, you probably recognized it as a parody or play on words form the classic family favorite, What About Bob?

Mark asked a hundred questions about the clouds, the speed of the airplane, and how high we were. He was amazed as he glanced out the window and saw the small specks he knew to be cars and trucks.

When we landed, Mark and I went to get our luggage, golf clubs, and then to get a rental car. As we drove off in the brand new Ford, he looked at me and grinned with an I-can't-believe-this-is-happening look on his face. I could tell our bond as father and son was about to deepen.

The first day we played two rounds of golf, and sometime during the second round, maybe the seventh hole, I sent Mark to get our cart, which we had left on the cart path. When he pulled up, I asked him where he had gotten the cart. He pointed in the general direction where we had left ours.

"Well Mark, the clubs on this cart are not ours." I turned and looked, and sure enough, here came two distraught golfers in my cart looking for their cart and clubs. I chuckled and gladly surrendered the spoil to its rightful owners. Mark and I laughed for at least thirty minutes. I enjoyed not feeling any pressure to treat him as if he had done something wrong.

If I had scolded him and told him he needed to watch what he was doing, what would I have gained? What would that have done for our relationship? Instead, we just had one royal laugh that lasted the entire weekend. And the story will become a part of our family lore.

The morning of my niece's wedding, everyone was scrambling around trying to fix this and fix that. Mark and I had spent the night in a mountain cabin in Cloudcroft, New Mexico. So before we could get tied up with the wedding party fixing whatever it was that needed last-minute-fixing, we took a drive to Camp Dale Resler, my old Boy Scout camp. The ranger was there and let us drive right on in.

We went to the old campfire grounds, and we looked for the totem pole I had helped design and build some twenty-five years earlier. Sure enough, there she stood—tall and stoic with my name carved right where I had left it all those years earlier.

Mark got a little tear in his eye. "Thanks for bringing me here, Dad. I always knew you were a boy once, but I feel somehow like I'm sharing that part of your life with you." He put his arm around me. "It's really cool to see something you built twenty-five years ago as a boy, and to see it still standing here, after all the rain, snow, and other kids."

My eyes welled up and I hugged him tightly.

We found an out-of-the-way restaurant and had a terrific breakfast. We talked about nothing but fun stuff. Then we headed over to the golf course so we wouldn't be late for our tee-time. The course was at the same resort where the wedding was to take place, so we couldn't get into too much trouble or be too late. After another eighteen holes, we drove straight to our cabin, changed clothes, went to the wedding, kissed and hugged everyone, and took off again.

The whole weekend was a once in a lifetime opportunity to draw close to my son and for my son to draw close to me. God blessed us with a very special time together, and years later; Mark still remembers the trip and all the details.

Kevin Paul Mullaney

When my son, Kevin, turned nine, he wanted to go on a business trip with me and then take a few days at the beach on Galveston Island to go deep-sea fishing in the Gulf of Mexico. We flew to Houston, Texas, rented a Mustang convertible and drove to the hotel. First order of business was to present a business seminar at the downtown conference center.

The next morning as we got dressed, I noticed that Kim had packed Kevin with a suit that was identical in color and style to mine. What a hoot. This had to be one of my most proud moments with Kevin. I felt like a showoff walking through the conference center next to him. He may have been the very first mini-me.

While we were standing at an elevator, I noticed he kept looking up at my double-breasted suit and then he would look down at his double-breasted suit. I'm convinced he was proud of himself because every time he checked out his new duds, his little nose would flare out. I had to turn my head so he wouldn't see me laughing. Eventually I decided to do the exact same thing. Check him out, check me out, and then dramatically flare my nostrils. We finally connected on this and had a great belly laugh that continues to this day.

I introduced Kevin as my assistant. Throughout my seminar, Kevin bolted into character and was spot on all day. You would have thought he had been doing this forever, or at least had some thorough training. Neither would be true. Kevin just has always had a certain business savvy that comes so naturally. He managed to put the entire program into his own perspective and then did his best to anticipate my every move and beat me to the next task.

He had never seen an overhead projector nor operated a slide projector in sequence with a presentation. I never had to give him one instruction on either piece of equipment. As a child, he would look at just about anything and rather than read the instructions, grab it and go. This is a bit scary because, that is too close to home and identical to my personality.

Every student in the seminar expressed the joy they felt in watching a father and son working together like a well-greased comedy machine. It may not have been the smoothest seminar I ever delivered in my professional career, but it was certainly the most exciting and memorable.

When we headed to the restaurant for a business dinner, his masculine instincts took over. He grabbed the menu and without out reservation or permission, ordered the steak and lobster. I was not entirely surprised since Kevin was always testing his boundaries. He knew if he went too far, I would reel him back a little. Not this time however, he was one of the guys just hanging out after a long successful day. A man's gotta do what a man's gotta do.

Usually I would steer my kids to choose something less expensive. Plus, I generally had the kids drink water to save a few dollars. Not on a business dinner apparently. Besides, the company was footing the bill so Kevin surmised. He needed something a little stronger than water.

"Strawberry float please." Kevin exclaimed.

I don't recall what he ordered for dessert and I have no idea if he cleared his plate. I remember clearly however, that he was having a great time and he was definitely my son. In the morning, we put the top down on the convertible and Kevin jumped over the side landing correctly in his seat. Who was this kid?

Having lived in Galveston twice before our trip, I knew the people to call to arrange the deep-sea fishing excursion. Large party boats take maybe a hundred people at a time and are more affordable than a charter fishing trip, so we decided to try it out.

We left the docks before sunrise and returned at sundown. I have pictures of Kevin and me baiting our hooks, covered in squid juice, ketchup, mustard and sweat. We fought giant waves, slippery decks, a heavily rocking boat, sick fishermen two slots down, triggerfish, and rumors of the big one that got away. By the end of the day, Kevin had bagged over 75 pounds of fresh Gulf Coast Red Snapper. We had our photo taken in front of the great catch and then proudly gave the fish away to those less fortunate. I was so proud of how independent Kevin was. He never slowed me down. In fact, I had a hard time keeping up with him.

The captain of the boat invited us into his quarters and let Kevin sail the ship. I took dozens of pictures of Kevin sitting behind the captain's wheel and tried to catch him not smiling, but had no such luck. His white wrinkled swabbie cap made him look similar to Gilligan from the television show, Gilligan's Island.

This trip with Kevin was a glimpse of who he was going to be. Kevin goes full throttle in everything he does. When he works, he is completely in overdrive and not easily diverted. When he is in the playing mode or enjoying gear, he is running full out with no regrets or interference form other obligations.

Kevin and I still talk about that trip and it will always remain one of the best mental snapshots of our time of bonding. The nose-flaring thing has fortunately not stopped!

Matthew James Mullaney

Matthew wanted to go to Galveston Island as well, but he wanted to hit as many fun events as possible. While we were driving from Houston to Galveston, we were on the causeway south on the interstate heading toward the Gulf of Mexico. Matthew grew silent, seeming to be lost in thought. As he stared out the window at a bridge construction project, he squirmed in his seat, giggled, twitched, scratched his head, and finished with folded arms and a very content look upon his face. I wanted to know what Matthew had internalized.

"Matthew, what are you doing?" I asked.

He snickered just a little. "I just figured out how they pour wet concrete into a steal pipe that goes to the bottom of the bay."

Matthew spent the next hour explaining the entire engineering project. I was blown away. He was nine years old, lived in the country, played in the mud, and had never seen a construction project bigger than the ones he'd designed in his little brother's sandbox.

As we closed in on Galveston Island, Matthew made it clear that he had already conceived and planned every moment of everyday and how we were going to spend them. If something he had planned was not available, he had a Plan B.

We did water slides, jet skis, ferryboats, and Popeye's Chicken. Eating was necessary, but I got the vibe that Matthew didn't want to spend too much time in a restaurant. In Matthew's mind and heart, it was time to play and he expected me to keep up. After the first day I was so tired and sore, I almost took a timeout the next day. But, this moment was not about me, it was about us and in Matthew's world, he didn't want to miss one moment. Somewhere I must have a T-shirt that say's, "I survived Matthew's nine-year-old trip."

When Matthew walks into the room, even when it is filled with unfamiliar visitors, he brings a peaceful joy with him. It was not uncommon for him to make eye contact with a six-foot adult and shout out, "Howdy neighbor." He is simply wired to work when it is time to work, rest when it is time to rest, and to totally play when it is time to play.

As our weekend came to an end, we decided to fish all night long on the 91st Street fishing pier. I had worked at this pier many years earlier when I was in college. The moment was a bit surreal for me. Growing up, my family was card-carrying members of that pier. I had fished from that pier hundreds of times. On that particular day, Matthew and I stood in the same spot my father and I fished nearly twenty years earlier.

Fortunately, we were blessed with a very fruitful night of fishing. Nobody else on the pier was noticeably catching fish that night. Many of those on the pier tried getting closer to us but it made no difference for them. Only Matthew and I were reeling them in! The good news for the other folks that night was that Matt and I had a plane to catch so we gave away a very generous number of sand trout.

As the sun was beginning to peak over the waters edge, Matthew turned toward me. "Dad, this is pretty cool! Fishing all night long on the exact pier you worked at when you were here in college and in the same exact spot where you and Grandpa Mullaney fished twenty years ago. I don't know how you felt fishing with your dad, but I really like this. Yeah, I could do this some more!"

My lungs filled with fresh morning air, my heart began pounding, my jaw muscles began to quiver, and my eyes swelled with tears as I hugged my son. "Matthew, I love fishing with you here. This is a life-changing moment for me. You've given me a special gift."

"What is that, Dad?"

"Being here with you all night helps me understand the love my father must have felt for me when we stood in the same spot all those years ago. I had forgotten about my time here with him. Thank you for that special moment, Matthew. I will never forget it."

Matthew never met his Grandpa Mullaney. So when he made the remark about fishing on the same pier that I had fished with my father, I realized the loss he felt by never having met my dad—perhaps even deeper than he did.

Kristin Rose Mullaney

When my daughter Kristin reached the age of nine, I became acutely aware that her choices, while similar to the boys, came with understandable differences. Like two of her older brothers, Kristin chose a convertible for the trip. She didn't want to fly; she wanted to take the drive. She wanted to go to Galveston Island, but was more interested in fancy hotels, fancy restaurants, jewelry shopping, and mall visits, than she was baiting fishhooks and catching crabs.

The perfect day for my daughter was sleeping late, having breakfast brought to the room on a tray, sunning by the pool, swimming, floating on a raft, and then lunch on the beach. After lunch, it was time to shower, do her hair, shop at the mall on the mainland, and hit an afternoon matinee. For dinner it was lump crabmeat at Gaido's.

Metaphorically speaking, I was struggling for air at times. I tried loosening my shirt collar but found no relief. So with great excitement and all the marketing savvy I could muster, I suggested a few father-daughter things like water slides, jet skis, wave diving, and digging holes in the sand. She had mercy on me and away we went, creating memories that will last a lifetime.

Once we got to the water slide, I realized that I may have been better off at the mall. LOL. Kristin would come blazing down the slide screaming all the way to the bottom. She wouldn't stop to catch her breath. She would run back up the very long staircase to do it all again. She easily hit the slide three times to my once. I made the quick decision that I was out gunned on this amusement. I would rather pay for more time on the Jet Ski than have a heart attack climbing those stairs trying to keep up with a nine year old!

I drove Kristin around on the Jet Ski just long enough for her to realize that she wanted the controls. Before I could maneuver to the back of the two-man seat, she depressed the gas and I went flying off the side into the water. Uncharacteristically, I came up out of the water laughing. She was so sorry...at least that is what she led me to believe. Once I assured her that I was ok, she caught the mood and we had a great laugh. Turns out, that wouldn't be the last time I was ejected from the watercraft.

Unlike the boys, Kristin wanted to take long walks in the sand at the waters edge. Searching for shells and just enjoying the sunset reminded me so much of her mother. What a little lady I had on my hands. Even with an overwhelming population of male species at home, she celebrated her feminine side and the sweetness of her smile melted my heart.

I will never forget how important it was for Kristin to get all dressed up and go out to a classy restaurant on Seawall Boulevard. As I noticed her unbroken smile across the dining room table, I could see her mother's reflection in her tiny little face. Kristin was already becoming a young lady and had so many of her mother's mannerisms. As she ordered her meal, her legs rocked back and forth since they couldn't touch the floor. I loved how she would correct me for being silly and trying to bamboozle her. I realized on my trip with Kristin that she was going to be a real handful. I would have to bring my "A" game because the young boys would be calling soon. I've always told Kristin, "It is a good thing that you have older bigger brothers." I don't think she understood what I was saying until she reached her teens.

I thought Kristin would be so tired that she would sleep all the way home. Didn't happen. She wrote in her journal, read me a book and made sure that I wouldn't fall asleep. She bought a gift for each of her brothers and mother to let them know she was thinking about them during her vacation. For herself, she bought some earrings and a matching necklace. I thank God for this time with her.

Kenneth Daniel Mullaney

By the time Kenneth reached the age of nine, our family was spread out between Rockwall, Texas, and Albuquerque, New Mexico. I had taken a new pastoral job at a church in Albuquerque and was working on transitioning my family there.

As I mentioned earlier, Kenneth had an inner instinct to watch and learn from his older siblings. He too had been planning his trip for some time. He made a note that his brothers, his sister, and I had enjoyed four-day trips. At the time, I was commuting between Albuquerque and Rockwall and was temporarily holed up in a place Kenneth had never been. He also made a note of my new Honda Rodeo SUV and that I was staying in a brand new condo. And so the call came.

"Dad, this is Kenneth."

"Hi buddy, how are you?"

"I've been thinking . . . you owe me a nine-year-old trip . . . don't you?"

"Yes, I suppose I do."

"I think I have a plan to save you some money."

"What do you have in mind?" I will never forget his exact words.

"I would like to come out to Albuquerque and I am looking at staying around ten days."

He explained how I wouldn't need to rent a car or hotel and that we wouldn't need to eat out all the time. In great detail he told me all the things we could do together. My heart was jumping with excitement. What a treat.

"You strike a hard bargain Kenneth, but I think we can pull this off."

During the ten days, he was mostly interested in simply spending time with me. So many times I would catch Kenneth just watching and listening as I communicated with the staff at church. Following these brief meetings he would ask many questions.

Kenneth was so relaxed. If I asked him what he wanted to do, he would respond with answers like, "What do you usually do?" In the evenings he would cook Ramen noodles with canned chicken for the both of us. We would prop our pillows on the headboard, turn on the television, and watch old movies we selected from a video library at the condo office downstairs. Sometimes we played cards or just sat and talked for hours.

One day I surprised Kenneth with a day of golf. We played three separate courses for a total of 54 holes. It was a grand slam golf day. That was the first time and last time I ever played that much golf in one day. We finished with Der Wiener Schnitzel and enjoyed beef chilidogs, fries, and cokes. Then Kenny surprised me. The animated movie: "Monsters, Inc." had just hit the big screen. We stood in line for the opening night and then went back two more times. I loved this time with him. I never wanted him to leave. I realized how much I missed my family during this yearlong commute.

My takeaway from these ten days was how mature and caring Kenneth had become at the tender age of nine. He was taking responsibility for cooking the Ramen noodles with the can of chunked chicken added. He was even on his game with the crackers and butter. I know, this was not a health conscience meal by any stretch of the imagination but it was warm and fun just the same. He could tell story after story about family events that I thought he was too young to even notice.

When Kenneth headed back to Dallas, I felt the empty place in my heart that I had placed on hold from my emotions. I had convinced myself that this commute was the only way to keep my job and afford my children the opportunity to finish the school year with their friends. It was a very heavy price to pay.

How To Respond

How could I ever forget the Christmas day that Kenneth's older brother Matthew assembled his new rocket and left it, primed, on the launching pad in the den right next to the fireplace. Kenneth was simply being his age when he launched the rocket into the den ceiling. It blasted off with flames, smoke, and a trail of fire—eventually landing in the dining room when the parachute popped out. The house filled with smoke as Kim screamed to the top of her lungs.

I lunged through the door after hearing all the commotion. After I realized that the coast was clear, meaning, no burning buildings and nobody hurt, I ran over to hold a now very upset and scared young boy in my arms. I taught him the urgency of the situation but his acceptance of the humor involved would not sink in immediately. We still chuckle at this Polaroid moment today.

Thank God, no one was hurt and no real damage was done. Unfortunately, being so young and being so scared, it took Kenneth several years before he came to the maturity level to laugh about it, which he does now. Love that moment Kenny!

Families have ample opportunities to become angry or to find the humor in accidents. It has taken me years to learn the proper response. I do my best to look on the brighter side these days. But it was not always that way. Once when Kevin, Kristin and I were on a youth trip to Colorado, I failed to respond correctly. I come from a long line of over-reactors and am very good at it MYSELF. (Someone in my family will no-doubt read this and shout; OVER-REACTOR!) LOL.

The youth camp was a small retreat that grouped several building in order to facilitate sleeping, group meetings and meals. While we were gathered in the main room on the very first night, the facility coordinator asked if anyone had seen the television set? Normally it sits in view of the whole room for special presentations or group videos. It was the only television available at the camp. Nobody took responsibility for the missing TV.

As we began searching, we located the TV fairly quickly. We found it in the boys dorm positioned at the foot of one of the bunks so that the new owner could play video games and watch movies. This shouldn't have been any surprise. Meaning the boy's dorm verses the girl's dorm. The surprise came as we learned that my son, Kevin, had procured the television. I was the new associate pastor and the unknown factor in the group. The senior pastor blew a gasket and asked me if this was going to continue to be a problem. Little did he know, his son was Kevin's accomplice!

I regret today that I chose to humiliate and embarrass my son in front of all his new friends. I did not respond to the situation rather, I reacted. My family had just joined me in Albuquerque after being separated for one full year. Kevin had just left his high school friends as he was about to begin his senior year and he was making all new friends. I was the new associate pastor and was a bit nervous about everything. Still, I have played this video many times in my head and each time I conclude, that I could have handled this matter with much greater love, admiration and respect for Kevin. Publicly and honestly, I'm so sorry Kevin.

In high school, a young man decided to steal a kiss (on the cheek) from my daughter Kristin while she was walking up a set of stairs. A new form of social media had just surfaced. So when her brothers found out what had happened they used that media to find him. They discovered who he was, what he looked like, and where he lived. Then they went to have a brief chat with this guy. For the next two years this young kissing bandit went out of his way to avoid my daughter. This happened organically. I never said a word to my boys. I didn't have too. Their response was appropriate. Quietly I was so blessed.

We are all far from perfect and on a journey with plenty of learning curves. The key factor especially when raising kids is to try and see every challenge through the lenses of love, acceptance, grace, mercy, kindness, patience, and humor. Remain resolute about the value of the relationships God has divinely given you. Most importantly, guard your children. Always cover, protect, and encourage them. Be a rock for them, a safe place for their occasional retreats from life events and challenges. Do it with open arms no matter the circumstances.

Life Lessons

It's very challenging for me to watch a movie that is filmed and developed all within the confines of one space or room. Years ago, I watched a movie that did just that. Talk about a cheap budget film! The main actor was stuck in a phone booth for the entire movie. The plot was something about death and destruction if this guy in the phone booth did not follow all the instructions from the unknown voice on the other end of the phone. Somehow, they built suspense and a story around this scenario. However, at this point, I have absolutely no idea what the movie was about. My only real memory is this guy standing in a phone booth and talking you through the entire story on a pay phone.

Life happens differently for each of us everyday. It seems to come at us in varying seasons and chapters. The harder seasons last too long and the better seasons seem to fleet so quickly. We do our best to prolong the good times but none-the-less, they too slip through our grip as we try to hold on to them.

When I consider my primary schooling years from first grade through twelfth, I possibly attended class over 2,000 times. I really enjoyed Scouts, where I attended hundreds of meeting, events and campouts over an eight-year period. I held down several jobs that used up untold hours of my personal time. None of which, will I ever see again.

In the grander scale of my total years lived, I have been awake, breathing, and surviving this life for over 20,000 days. However, I've learned that each day of my life has one thing in common. Since time marches on and routine things we do to live blend together, it becomes impossible to distinguish one day from the next. As we search our thoughts, we realize that life boils down to two things, moments and memories.

Unless we intentionally create great moments and memories, our life story can become blurred by daily similarities and we can end up like the guy in the phone booth. Without remarkable moments in time, life may feel a bit like the movie, *Ground Hog Day*. Some great memorable moments are spontaneous and awesome while others are intentional.

I decided early as a father that I would do my best to create many awesome moments and memories for my family. This would create a wealth of value intended as a source of inner strength from which to draw from during hard times. I like to say that life comes down to moments and memories.

Laugh at the scary moments when fire-powered rockets are launched into your den ceiling. Soak up all the love you are receiving while your kids are handing it out freely. Take the necessary time to create moments that will build memories and character in each of your children. These positive memories will help generate confidence in your children and you will be blessed by the amazing personalities that emerge.

Kim and I used to allow the kids to jump under the covers with us on stormy nights or anytime they were scared. As the family grew, rather than telling the brood to go back to their own rooms, we just bought a bigger bed. I knew that we wanted to receive everything our kids had to offer us while they were handing it out. I also knew, the day would come when we couldn't pay them enough to cuddle up with mom and dad. Actually, that's a good thing...LOL

Chapter 5
How My Dad Shaped Me

Dad's Sacrificial Heart

My father served our country in the military until I was twelve. Many differences existed between our family's lives and those of civilians. My family moved twenty-six times in twenty-five years, from city to city and school to school. Of course I was not there for all of the moves, but by the time I graduated from high school, I had attended eleven different schools. The United States Army owned my dad, and it could do whatever it wanted with him.

His sacrificial example taught me the value of giving your life to the endeavor of serving others. His love for our country and the freedoms it has afforded us resounds even today, in my very being. Within my daily choices to serve and love our Father God, by serving and ministering to others, is the foundation of my dad's commitment and faithfulness to God, country, and family.

The memories I have of my dad are a bit fragmented. He was a very interesting combination of Marine drill sergeant, Army warrant officer, and Irish Catholic family man. He had lost his dad when he was thirteen and his mother allowed him to join the Marines when he was seventeen.

Most of what I can remember about dad from my youth is related to work or to occasions when he was having a good time with his Army buddies, friends, and family. I didn't really mind because he and my mother were good about letting us be a part of the festivities. We were rarely excluded from anything, especially in our home.

When I was nine, the Army sent my father to Thule, Greenland, which is basically the North Pole. So I didn't see him for one full year. With no phones, Internet or cell phones, my parents only option to kept in touch was by sending small reel-to-reel tapes back and forth. Every now and then my mom would allow my siblings and me to hear them.

Late at night, when Mom would listen to these tapes alone, I would peek around the door and watch as she cried when she heard my dad's voice. I didn't understand fully what she was going through. When I heard Dad's voice, it made me happy! Sometimes, she would listen to the tape over and over. I would pray for my father and mother because they really loved each other and being separated was difficult on both of them.

Impartation From My Father

While my childhood memories are a bit scattered, some things actually stuck in my heart. My father was an Irishman. Our family heritage was important to him. We grew up believing there was something special about our surname: Mullaney! Maybe it was the way Dad would say it after a few beers, but to me, I was never to bring shame or embarrassment upon the family name. That made a lasting impression on me and directly impacted many of my personal choices. I hope I have expressed that same family value to my children.

Mom and Dad were always hugging or kissing one of us. I remember going through a phase right after hair started growing under my arms, when I wasn't exactly comfortable with a kiss from my dad, especially in public. During my high school years I chose wrestling as my sport. In my senior year I thought I was pretty cool. Right after I won a major citywide wrestling tournament, my dad headed my way.

Oh my Lord, here he comes. He's going to lay one on me right in front of all my friends. He gave me a kiss right smack on the lips (pretty normal in those days) in front of God and everybody. He followed that with a huge bear hug. "That's my boy! You did great, Mark. I'm so proud of you."

Later in the locker room, one of my friends walked over to me. I knew I was about to be blasted. How humiliating. These guys were going to eat me alive.

"Mark, you are pretty lucky to have your dad come to your wrestling match," my teammate said. "I wish my dad would come to see me wrestle." The next thing he said really put a stranglehold on my attitude. "You know, my dad has never hugged me or kissed me in my whole life that I am aware of. Does your dad hug you all the time?"

I went straight home and gave my dad a huge hug and thanked him for coming to see me wrestle. Then I looked him in the eye. "Dad, you can hug me and kiss me anytime you want to." For the rest of his life, that's what he did.

Another notable moment occurred while I was at my parents twenty-fifth wedding anniversary. The adults were dancing in one of the rooms. Back in those days, a man would tap on another man's shoulder and that was the signal that they wanted to cut in and dance. I watched as a woman tapped on the shoulder of my dad's dance partner and began dancing with him. I didn't think anything of it until abruptly, my dad placed both hands on top of her shoulders and pushed her a full arms length away.

He pulled his right hand back slightly and pointed his index finger right smack in her face and delivered a very convincing rejection. The lady fled to the other side of the room and my dad walked over and planted a big kiss on my mom's lips and then he put his arm around her. My take-a-way from this moment was my father's response to something that was obviously wrong. His immediate actions have sustained me for years. He made a covenant with my mom and that would never be broken. This one event cemented my awareness of his true character.

Even with the fuzzy recall I have of childhood memories, my father's reputation and character remain very intact in my heart. I appreciate now when I hear my mom say; "you are so much like your father"! I have realized through the years that my father and my mother impacted my life in profound ways. Due to God's plan and divine connection with them, we become a reflection of their lives, character, strengths and weaknesses.

Dad's Final Six Months

When I was eighteen years old, my parents and younger brother Tim moved to Galveston Island. It's a barrier reef Island located fifty miles south of Houston, Texas in the Gulf of Mexico. I had remained in El Paso to continue my education at the University of Texas in El Paso. Six months after they moved, I rejoined my family for the summer and perhaps one semester at the local college.

I had no idea this would be my last six months with my father. In fact, none of us have any guarantee that we will ever see our loved ones ever again after they drive off in their cars of fly off in an airplane. By the grace of God, it was such a wonderful time for most of my family. Some of my siblings did not have that last six months with dad. But this brief time was unlike any I can remember.

This season was filled with boating, fishing, cooking out, and playing games. By spending so much time with my father during his last chapter on earth, I met a man I had never really known. I fell in love with my dad that summer. Of course, I always loved my dad, but it was at this time that I really got to know him. Growing up, it was rare for my father to sit with me and just share his thoughts, expectations, or his own life lessons. Most of my memories of my father are filled with working, building, fixing, cleaning, or getting into trouble.

I was working at Todd's Shipyard. I chose the graveyard shift so I could attend college during the day. One night my father stayed awake until 4:00 a.m. because he was concerned about my safety.

He quite frankly saved my life by teaching me the dangers of the industrial work place. I worked a specialized job known as "below the bottom" (the oil pan) of a ship. Two days prior to Dad talking with me, I had passed out from the chemicals that I was required to use for my job.

Dad warned me "never to risk my life on a job regardless of what I am being asked to do." He taught me to use my own common sense at all times even if it meant walking off the job. I have never forgotten his advice. In fact, I shared that same message with each of my children as they entered the work place.

I thank God that my family and I had such a significant time together in Galveston. This season of remarkable memories was truly a gift from God. We all slowed down and enjoyed each other before my father's final hour arrived.

Dad's Last Moments

My brother, Charlie, and brother-in-law, George, worked tirelessly to revive dad the evening he had a series of heart attacks. They were able to do so briefly. After calling for the ambulance, I held my father's head in my lap and cried out loud each time he would die in my arms. My brother and George kept dad breathing long enough for the ambulance to arrive. As they rolled up with their lights flashing and their sirens squealing, my dad motioned to me to come closer. As I listened closely he said in my ear;

"Take my watch with you, I don't want those b****rds (sorry, that was my dad) to steal it!" LOL. I still have his watch today.

I rode in the ambulance with dad while Charlie and George went home to tell my mom and sister Della what had happened and get everyone to the hospital.

I stood outside the door to the emergency room where the doctors were doing their best to save dad's life. The door to the emergency room flew open and they were rolling my dad to the cardiac unit upstairs. I grabbed a hold of the gurney and kept up with everyone running to the elevator. Once on the elevator, my father asked the doctor to loosen his belt because he was having difficulty breathing. The doctor, while very concerned for my father's life said;

"It's not your belt that's making it hard to breath."

Then the doctor looked at me and shook his head as if to say;

"It won't help."

I could really care less about everything the doctor understood about Dad's situation at this point. A dying man felt like this might help. I reached over and loosened my father's belt and he smiled back at me and said;

"Thanks son. Feels better already."

Turns out, that was my father's last request for me and the last complement I ever heard him utter. I loved it when he called me son. That meant he was my father. I regret not having taken this moment to say out loud; "I love you Dad!" I was afraid if I had used this moment to express my feelings, he might have surmised that I feared his death. I did not want him worrying about my feelings at this critical moment. Besides, he already knew that my love for him was intact.

My dad went by the name Chuck. He was a strong willed Irishman. I believe that Dad stayed alive just long enough to look into my mom's eyes one more time before he had to say goodbye. As my family gathered outside the ICU cardiac unit, we prayed and prayed for dad's recovery. The doctors told us that my father continued having several full cardiac arrests. They said he would literally die, but with the tools the doctors had in 1975, they were able to bring him back within minutes.

The doctor came into the hall to give us the bad news that dad was not doing well. My mom asked if she would be able to see him. The doctor was shocked to learn that she had not already done so. He immediately ushered her to my father's bedside. My father woke immediately. He looked into my mother's eyes, took her by the hand and said:

"Hi babe!"

Then he closed his eyes for the very last time. The doctors could do nothing to bring him back after he had seen my mom. Dad was gone. For some reason, as we all were leaving the hospital, the nurse came to me and handed me a small brown paper bag and said; "here, you'll want these." Confused, I opened the bag and looked inside. It was my dad's things. Right on top was his shorts and the belt I had earlier loosened for him. Suddenly, it was hard for me to breath.

God builds character in hard times. I woke the next morning missing my dad and faced with the reality that I had been given the responsibility of breaking the news to my younger brother Tim. A friend drove me to West Columbia, Texas where Tim was serving as a staff member at the local scout camp. Unsuspecting of any problems, he greeted me with hugs and cheers. He was fifteen and finishing his Eagle Scout award. Because of this tragedy, Tim never had the chance to finish what he clearly earned.

When he first saw me walk up to the class he was teaching, he was excited to see me. He smiled so big and asked:

"What the heck are you doing up here?"

I tried to speak but no words would come out of my mouth. All I could do was hug him with all my strength. He realized something was up so I asked him if we could go somewhere and talk. We sat on the edge of a picnic table amidst the warm sun and tall pine trees. I had to dig really deep to find the right words to say. I didn't want to deliver this message but had no choice. Tim would be crushed.

This was an excruciating moment in my life. For years I internalized the pain I felt seeing the bewilderment and shock on my little brother's face. Our Father God says:

"He turns all things to the good for those who love Him."

In other words, God will take the hardest of times in our lives and use them to generate inner strength, hope, and resolve.

We headed to Tim's tent to pack all his gear and to the office to sign him out of camp. Rather than talking, we both cried the entire time. It was the longest drive home of my life. My friend Robert drove for us because we were in no condition to do so. He too loved my father and wrestled with his own emotions but stayed strong and compassionate.

Following the funeral at Ft Bliss, we headed back to Galveston to pack up our things and relocate everyone back to El Paso, Texas. When I walked into the apartment that overlooked our boat dock and Offatts Bayou, I felt bewilderment. Everything had changed so quickly. Just a week earlier, we were sitting at the dining room table enjoying my father's last meal...fried chicken, mashed potatoes, and green beans.

My greatest moment of brokenness came as I began packing my father's personal things. I was trying to reconcile his death while putting all of his clothing into boxes. The closet smelled like him and I could remember his smile when he was wearing each of his business suits and shirts. Suddenly, his bowling ball mysteriously rolled across the floor lodging against my foot.

When I picked up the ball, I saw "Chuck" embossed across the front. My heart sank as it did when the nurse at the hospital handed me the brown paper bag filled with his things. I stood and wept for quite a while and the same questions I had at the hospital persisted. "Who will wear these clothes? Who will use this bowling ball? What happens now? Not only was my father gone, but also his personal possessions were no longer needed.

Years later, while serving our local police department as a chaplain, I possessed an inner strength that gave me a heart of compassion when I had to deliver many such messages. I was divinely prepared since that day with my brother. God has used me to help so many families handle such tragic news.

My Fathers Legacy

My father's character and strength made distinct impressions on the people who knew him. Years following his death, I was the benefactor of his contributions and work ethic. Soon after Kim and I got married, I made the decision to postpone my college for a few years due to financial stress. Kim was enrolled at Texas Woman's University and doing quite well studying Occupational Therapy. I had bounced around with my degree program a few times and made the deans lower list twice. Meaning, twice removed from college due to poor grades and lack of focus. I still have copies of my letters to the dean begging him to allow me to return to my studies.

I studied cartography for one semester during my first three years at UTEP in El Paso. It barely qualified me for an entry-level position as a draftsman. But at least I could go from a construction job to a professional status in an office building. I was now responsible for my new commitment to solely support both of us while Kim completed her degree.

Many years earlier following my father's retirement from the military, he went to work for Southern Union Gas Company in El Paso, Texas. He too started at an entry-level job just to get his foot in the door as he began his second career. He quickly moved through their ranks and was promoted to an executive position in Galveston, Texas just prior to his passing. The home office for this company was located in downtown Dallas, Texas. Since I lived in the Dallas area, and my father had worked for this company, I submitted my first job application as a draftsman. Frankly, it was the only job they offered that I might just slightly be qualified for.

Note to self; due to the work ethic and impression my father had established with this company, I was hired right away. It most certainly was not about my qualifications. On the first day on my new job, while sitting at my very complicated drafting table, a senior executive by the name of Tony Prasil took an elevator from the top floor of this high-rise building to the bottom floor where I worked. He stood beside my desk and introduced himself.

"Hi, I'm Tony Prasil and you are Chuck's boy! So happy to meet you"!

He reached towards me, I stood to my feet, and we shook hands. I was so blown away. My boss sprang from his office to see what was going down.

Immediately after introducing himself, he told me that my father "Chuck" had impressed him so much while he was with the company that he personally wanted to meet me. He told me that they already had plans for me since they felt that some of that same measure of excellence my father had must have rubbed off on me. I was uncharacteristically speechless. Mr. Prasil was a man of stature. An impressive successful executive. He was very intelligent and when he spoke, people listened. He invited me to lunch and took me to the most expensive restaurant I had ever seen. My boss was not invited. Oops!

This was a divine encounter that God had arranged. I sat for over and hour listening to Mr. Prasil talk. He told me of the many contributions my father had made with regard to operations and cutting expenses. But mostly, he spoke of my father's integrity, ethics, and character. Then he seemed to zero in on me. He spent much of our time drilling me on my personal desires and goals. He wanted to do what he could to help me move along in the company. This was Mr. Prasil's way of showing his appreciation for my father. Blessing Chuck's son. I did work hard for my promotions. It was however apparent, that I had found favor with this company due to the life of my father.

"May the favor of the Lord our God rest on us; establish the work of our hands for us-- yes, establish the work of our hands." (Psalm 90:17 NIV).

If we will stop taking all the credit for our personal accomplishments and learn to thank God for His favor, we may go further than we ever dreamed possible.

Life Lessons
The way we choose to live our life today will be remembered and revisited by the many good friends we develop along the way.

Technology is developing all around us. I have reached a logical conclusion for co-existing with this electronic matrix. Live your life as if you are always being filmed or recorded. I see clips on YouTube, Facebook and even the news all the time depicting unsuspecting people doing foolish things on digital recording devices. All of these "Polaroid" moments are being captured on little spy cameras. The newly discovered stars of these public films all have the same blown away response; "I didn't know I was being taped"! LOL.

When I look back over life with my father and all the fond memories I have, I realize that even as a child, I had my little spy camera running. We may never realize it fully, but our children are eyewitnesses to the life we live and they are responders to the examples we set.

Children become a reflection of the father who thought he could hide. This is also true of the mother. God's word and society teaches us that our children receive their identity from their father. They carry on the family name, crest and bloodline. Even if the father chooses to not be present in the lives of their offspring. Too often, children are forced to live without both a mother and a father. Remember, that little spy cameras are running in the hearts and minds of all children. They learn more by our example than from the words we speak. An absent, disconnected, and missing father or mother will effect their children in an adverse manner.

The greatest takeaway for me from my father has been through understanding how much he sowed into my life even when I did not realize he was making a deposit. I discovered over time that I was being shaped both good and bad by the relationship we had as I was growing up. His wisdom has returned to the forefront of my thoughts on many occasions.

How you decide to live your life will be revisited and evident in your child's personality, confidence, thoughts, and life choices.

Chapter 6
The Importance of a Hug

A Hug Supplies Life-Giving Energy

When I met Kim Latchaw in 1976, she was majoring in Occupational Therapy at Texas Woman's University, in Denton, Texas. Occupational Therapy helps people if they become dysfunctional in some manner due to an accident, disease, disability, aging, or birth defect. She was part of a woman's choir at the university, which toured communist (at the time) Romania. While she was there, she learned that the orphanages were overcrowded. She shared with me how concerned she was because little babies, if left completely alone throughout their infancy, can actually die from lack of affection.

I was shocked to learn that by giving affection to these infants, you actually pump life-giving energy into their spirit and body. The same is true regardless of our age. Everybody needs a hug. I am a big advocate of hugs and kisses. I believe the "hugger" gets as much affection, love, and assurance as the "huggee." I discovered a recent article that discusses some studies that confirms my original thinking. I have included it at the end of this chapter.

In conversation one day with my children, I decided to explore the idea of appropriate affection for my kids. Since I like working with numbers, I told my eleven-year-old son Matthew that he had probably been hugged and kissed more than 10,000 times in his lifetime. He was shocked by such a huge number and had the look of disbelief on his face. So we got out the calculator and tried to work up a good estimate. We started with just one hug a day from his mother and one from me.

At the time, Matthew was eleven years and six months old. That made him somewhere around 4,197 days old. If his mother and I each hugged him one time per day, then he would have received 8,395 hugs. And if we kissed him at the same time, which we usually do, he would have received an equal amount of kisses. At first, he thought I had overestimated a little bit.

"Wait a minute," I said. "During the past eleven years, how many times did you come and hug me and your mom?"

He thought for a moment. "Probably once per day, too."

That doubled the number of hugs and kisses to 16,790.

"What about your grandmother and your aunts and uncles? What about your pastor and our good friends of the family who come to visit?"

We thought for a minute and added another 2,500 and decided Matthew had received almost 20,000 hugs and an untold number of kisses. I asked him if he thought that was pretty accurate? He agreed.

"Matt, how many times per day do I actually hug you?"

He thought for a moment. "Four or five."

"What about your mom?"

"The same."

"Wow, Matthew! If that's correct, you may have already been hugged thirty to forty thousand times."

He was shocked.

"Well, I guess you won't be needing any more hugs will you?"

Matthew jumped into my lap, gave me a great big hug and exclaimed:

"I think I need lots more hugs",

In an article released in November 2014, Roger Dobson presents research that leans the direction of my personal beliefs. He says that studies show that daily cuddles can combat infections and lowers risk of heart disease. He states that hugging releases stress-reducing hormone oxytocin and that ten seconds of hugging a day can lower your blood pressure. He writes:

A hug or two a day may be more effective than an apple for keeping doctors at arm's length. Regular embraces can lower the risk of heart disease, combat stress and fatigue, boost the immune system, fight infections and ease depression, according to a new study.

Just ten seconds of hugging can lower blood pressure and after this time elapses, levels of feel-good hormones such as oxytocin increase, while the amounts of stress chemicals, including cortisol, drop.

The positive emotional experience of hugging gives rise to biochemical and physiological reactions, says psychologist Dr. Jan Astrom, who led the study report published in the journal Comprehensive Psychology.

A second study found that after ten seconds of hugging, levels of various hormones in men and women aged 20 to 49 changed. Oxytocin is secreted by the body during childbirth and in breastfeeding, where it stimulates release of milk. Until recently, its effects were thought to be confined to just that.

But research is increasingly showing that it seems to have many more effects, from improving social skills to combating stress and encouraging trust. The skin contains a network of tiny, egg-shaped pressure centers called Pacinian corpuscles that can sense touch and which are in contact with the brain through the Vagus nerve. The Vagus nerve winds its way through the body and is connected to a number of organs, including the heart. It is also connected to oxytocin receptors. One theory is that stimulation of the Vagus nerve triggers an increase in oxytocin, which in turn leads to the cascade of health benefits.[5]

Just my observation, but this sounds like a reasonable argument for the true value of breast-feeding.

Life Lessons

The love and closeness that a father shows to his children may never really show up in charts and grafts. Where it will show up is in the confidence and integrity displayed in the lives of his adult children. I believe the bible is true. One of the teachings we have is about training our children in the way that they should go. The bible promises us that if we are successful in doing this, our children will not depart from these teachings.

I have learned from experience that this promise does not mean that our children will not experience some turbulent times or make some bad decisions. I believe the Bible is saying that at the core of who they become, the principles we teach them will live inside their souls and in times of trouble, this truth will guide them to make better choices at some point in their future.

Teach children truth requires a trusting relationship between God, parents and their children. That trusting relationship begins at a very early age. The love and affection we show them daily is an emotional confirmation that we truly receive, accept, and love who they are as people. We are affirming their worth and value. They are as important to us as we are to them.

I've also learned that it is important to truly enjoy the things your children enjoy. They cannot always be doing what the adults like to do. I used to squeeze into the very small twelve-inch high plastic swimming pool, enjoy mud fights, and playing with the Tonka trucks in the sand box while smiling, and laughing the entire time. Kim would let them choose the meal for the family and then

---

[5] http://www.dailymail.co.uk/health/article-2230972/Embrace-hugging--good-you.html

help them prepare it. It some of the most fun and simple times that matter most.

Love is really measured by the amount of time we spend with our children giving, loving and sincerely enjoying each other.

Chapter 7
The Faster the Wheel Turns

Moving at the Speed of Life

Years ago, on a trip to Stockholm, Sweden, I had the great pleasure of being invited into the home of a dear friend to spend the evening with he and his family. They prepared a lovely dinner of authentic Swedish cuisine. We sat around the dining room table, no television running in the background, and enjoyed a wonderful meal without any pressure or time constraints. The meal simply lasted as long as it needed to last. Afterward, we retired to a sitting room where we enjoyed conversation and a snifter of Schnapps. (Google it).

I told the couple about the typical daily schedule my family and I kept. They were troubled at how young the busyness began for children in the United States and remarked how they believed it would eventually kill the family unit. Until then, I thought we were pretty normal. I hadn't really given much consideration to the fact that each of my children was on a wheel that seemed to be spinning faster and faster each year.

My friends in Sweden helped me to stop and realize that my family was out of balance. Maybe our lives really were moving at breakneck speed. Could it be that my family and I had fallen prey to the bumping and grinding of life in the States? I took a step back to evaluate everything we were doing as a family. Here's what our average day looked like before that awakening meal.

The Rat Race

At 6:30 a.m., the alarm sounded. By 6:45 we rolled out of bed and jumped into the shower. We got dressed and rushed through our breakfast. The kids made some sort of attempt at picking up a few items from their bedroom floors and then tossed their covers back on their beds. We rushed to the car and fought traffic to one more day of fun.

I'm not sure what lunchtime looked like for the kids, but from my perspective, I grabbed something quick, taking no more than thirty minutes, knowing that if I returned any later than that, my boss would rip my face off. I tried to finish my work in the afternoon, but if I didn't, I had to take it home.

When we arrived home, the kids finished cleaning the bedrooms, the dogs needed to be fed and let outside, all of us wanted a quick snack, then we split up to finish our work or homework. After dinner, we looked at the calendar to see what else we had to do that night.

If it was Monday night, the kids had to get ready for scouts. Tuesday night, they had baseball games. Wednesday night, they had church activities. Thursday nights were up for grabs. Friday nights included some sort of social activities or more sports activities. Saturdays were reserved for shopping, recitals, choir concerts, cheerleader practice and some sort of little league game. And so it went.

By the time our heads hit the pillow each night, we were consumed with thoughts about the next day, which looked pretty much the same.

Our schedule did not allow for creativity, deep thinking, real family time, or showing appreciation and respect for what we had. I know the pathway I had chosen was about providing for them. But my modus operandi begged the question; was this pathway healthy for them or our family as a whole?

Another factor existed, which I have not even entered into the above equation. Many statistics have been compiled revealing a shocking bit of information about what kids do with their spare time. You will see in a later chapter that the average child in America watches 5.11 hours of television each day.

How is this even possible? My children do not have this kind of free time in their schedules. Maybe some family structures are looser than mine. Perhaps study time or sleep time is being substituted for television time. Kim and I set parameters that all of us could live with. No television on school nights. I even adhered to that rule until all the kids were in bed. Then I would watch the news.

I understand that some children may never have an opportunity to live in a two-parent home. Some are abused, others are shuffled from school to daycare, and too many become latchkey kids fending for themselves daily. So I understand that many of my illustrations may not seem to connect to everyone. However, the one-on-one principles can amply apply to almost everyone. Hopefully, you will glean something to help strengthen and build your family—especially your children, our very next generation.

Is Life Really Speeding Up?

Life doesn't really speed up. How we choose to live life and how many activities we pack into one day can directly impact our availability to embrace each moment. The more activities we pack into any given span of time will create the feeling that things are just moving too fast. Fewer things to do will enhance involvement, commitment, and relaxation.

When I was a child, summer lasted much longer than it does now. Granted, we had more summer vacation days than we do now. We also had fewer programed activities. This made our days seem to last longer. School started after Labor Day, rather than in mid-August. We were afforded time to explore, create and discover. Half the fun we had was trying to decide what to do with all that time. Old pieces of lumber made pretty cool forts. Flat tires gave us a chance to use some tools. It also gave my parents some time to teach me responsibility. It was time to be together as a family.

My wife recalls having time to run and play after family dinner (no television) while her grandparents enjoyed sitting, watching, and sipping a cool iced tea on the front porch.

When I was a child, we actually had time as a family to sit down and enjoy a conversation while eating a home cooked meal. And when we received a letter from a friend or relative, we gathered in the living room to listen to Mom read it to us.

When the phone rang and my grandmother was calling from Louisville, Kentucky, my mom (Rosie) would shout loudly;

"Kids come quick! Grandma is on the phone and it's LONG DISTANCE!"

You would have thought something really major was happening. In those days, a long-distance call was a special moment and a big expense. It was also considered very special to hear from family so far away.

I'm not trying to sound old fashioned, nor am I advocating a return to the good ole' days, but we do need to find ways to spend more quality time together in the context of our modern culture. I have spent many hours contemplating the pace of life in our society and I have come to the following conclusion: time is the same as it has always been, but the demands on our time are much different.

A year has always been 365 days, plus a day during a leap year. That never changes. What has changed and will continue to change are you and me. This is the variable. A host of complex factors exist, and they can be managed once realized. Here is how it works:

When we reach our fifth year, we have lived for 1,825 days—and one year equals about one-fifth of our total life, or twenty percent. That is a pretty significant percentage. A five-year-olds memory is pretty limited, so practically everything discovered is new and exciting. Thus, one year is a rather significant piece of the pie as well as a large percentage of total time in existence.

When a person turns forty, he has survived roughly 14,600 days. One year later, he has lived 14,965 days. In this scenario, one year equals roughly two and half percent of his total life or one/fortieth of his total life.

The mind realizes the complex factors and files that chapter (year of life) into the memory. It logs repetitive actions, but eventually routine experiences end up running together and disappearing. I call this the "vacuum factor." Everything gets swept away, but where did it go?

Days and years only seem to get faster because each year becomes less of a percentage of the total pie. Many of our routine days are simply repeated events, and the vacuum factor treats these events as though they never existed, or it blends them without points of value. Thus, time disappears unless something significant occurs.

Recapturing Time

Many people say, "Do less, own less, download, and simplify your life." But this isn't the only formula for slowing down. Ironically, I think this formula oversimplifies the process. We must reduce our commitments outside of the family and reduce our toys (grown up toys and children's toys) so we can get more out of every moment. By doing so, I believe our memories will be much clearer and distinct.

The time we spend with our loved ones is much more significant than these other activities. My days are much more meaningful when I build a whole new set of memories with my family.

I carpeted the garage and organized it as safe place for my kids to explore the things they loved to do. I filled it with drums, guitars, a piano, P.A. system and microphones. As a family, we built one/eighth scale race cars, remote controlled airplanes, rockets, baseball fields with caged backstops, giant sand boxes, mud pits under the trampoline for "friendly" wrestling matches, rabbit cages, snake boxes, and duck cages. I impressed my kids with semi-safe giant bon-fires, ginormous fireworks displays, go-kart tracks, and doghouses. Yes, we even built swimming pools in creeks by erecting solid damns out of riverbed rocks. But most importantly, we built memories.

Preparing meals together is a good practical way to enjoy your family's company. Let your children plan a meal or two. Even let your older children play head chef. Kim would help in the kitchen and I would teach them how to grille outside over a hot bed of charcoal. Children need to contribute and feel value. Only parents can build this family bond.

Camping is another great way to build closeness as a family. It is a great escape from the day-to-day world of telephones, video games, and iPads. As you arrive at the campsite, lock all of your cell phones in the trunk. Once the camp is set up, make sure your schedule is completely blank. Plan for nothing more than meals and staying dry. This allows the entire family to participate with spontaneity, creativity, and individuality.

While we were living in Mexico we were learning a foreign language by scheduling time to listen to an instructional computer program together. As our Spanish improved, we began using our new language for everyday tasks. Kim placed written signs on household items to spark our memories and help us learn. The really great thing about us working together was that when we were given instructions in Spanish, one out of seven was bound to understand and then could explain it to rest of us. I call this family synergy. It creates a sense of community and family. Everyone needs to be needed and recognize that we can make a difference in the lives of others.

On of my greatest challenges in building and organizing our personal world was to provide options for my children to exercise their own creativity. I wanted them included in the project from planning to implementation. I waited often for a new idea from one of my children so that they would recognize the constructive side of their own imagination. Once they felt accepted, important, and critical to the mission, their ideas and creativity would flow like a river. I hope to repeat this with my grandchildren.

Less Is Best

My wife and I were determined to be more effective. We decided we could accomplish more for our children by doing less, buying less, and ridding ourselves of any and all obligations that could be deemed unnecessary. We've coined a slogan around our home: less is best. We have recognized that our direct involvement with our children in any type of activity, whether work or pleasure, would always create a more responsive, enthusiastic, and memorable event. For this less is best concept to succeed, it would have to start at an early age. That was not always easy. But setting the example was critical.

Leading means you have forged ahead and are being followed by at least one other interested party. By asking God to help us discern our priorities, as a family and as individuals, we are beginning to see the leaner, more targeted choices in our activities. We are seeking God's desired balance in our lives. The balance between:

"Be still before the LORD and wait patiently for him;   fret not yourself over the one who prospers in his way, over the man who carries out evil devices!" (Psalm 37:7)

"Therefore, since we are surrounded by so great a cloud of witnesses, let us also lay aside every weight, and sin which clings so closely, and let us run with endurance the race that is set before us." (Hebrews 12:1)

Life is not about "keeping up with the Joneses." It's about finding your balance and learning to be content. We realized we were not running a sprint. We are in a lifetime marathon. Marathon runners do not carry excess baggage during a race. In fact, they make a point of getting rid of excess weight prior to the race. Things that could be considered precious, like body hair and jewelry, are oftentimes removed. I agree, these silly mentions may be just a little extreme for our discussion, but the example of the discipline is necessary, especially if the runner intends to win the race.

Life Lessons

We chose to make a concerted effort to do less on the outside of our families and concentrate more heavily on the relationships God has clearly given us on the inside of our families. This type of dedication to each other can lead to rebuilding families while slowing the wheels from turning so quickly.

King Soloman (the wise), son of David, opens the book of Ecclesiastes with seemingly hopeless words. But I want to challenge you to learn the greater meaning.

"What does man gain by all the toil at which he toils under the sun? A generation goes, and a generation comes, but the earth remains forever. The sun rises, and the sun goes down, and hastens to the place where it rises. The wind blows to the south and goes around to the north; around and around goes the wind, and on its circuits the wind returns.

All streams run to the sea, but the sea is not full; to the place where the streams flow, there they flow again. All things are full of weariness; a man cannot utter it; the eye is not satisfied with seeing, nor the ear filled with hearing." (Ecclesiastes 1:3-8)

With my personality type, I have to work at accepting the words King Solomon spoke. Yet I decided that they were inspired by God and written by one of God's most wise men as an inspiration for all of us. God wants us to stop long enough to smell the roses rather than trying to replant all of them. Enjoy the people, times, family, and friends you currently have access to. Stop trying to change everything in a constant pursuit of your own happiness. Rather, enjoy the blessings God has already placed before you.

Children are only little and at home for a brief period of your life. As I comb through this book, which I began seventeen years ago, my children, so to speak, have come and gone. The opportunity I once had to daily interact with them is over. Trust me when I say, the time when your kids are with you at home will come and go more quickly than you can imagine. I am so thankful that God made me aware of this early into my fathering adventure. I am equally grateful that my wife, Kim was on board and encouraged wonderful family time.

Life is an adventure and raising kids is a gift. Put your whole heart into it and enjoy all of the moments that come your way. Slow the train down and offload excess cargo. Begin to experience the fullness of each family adventure. Create memories out of the moments that just happen. It does not always take money to make things happen. It just takes a wild imagination seeking an adventure and a willing heart.

Chapter 8
Respecting Authority

Everyone Answers to Somebody

I do not believe it is possible to live in complete harmony with yourself, your family, or your church until you settle the issue in your heart and mind that someone, somewhere, other than you, is in authority. The proper authority is there to help you. The same may also be true about those who mean to harm you. They may use their authority for their benefit regardless of the collateral damage to others. Discernment is so important.

If an individual is a business owner with millions of dollars in sales and thousands of employees, he still has to pay taxes; he has to report the required information pertaining to his personal earnings to the IRS, as well as the business transactions of his companies to his board, his stockholders and the IRS. Therefore, even rich guys are subject to those who are in authority over them.

Even if you believe you have eliminated all possible levels of human authority over you and you are completely autonomous with no designated individual who is in authority over you, you always, without exception, are accountable to God, Jesus, and His Holy Spirit—and, unfortunately, the IRS.

According to Webster's New Twentieth Century Dictionary, authority means "the power or right to command, act, enforce obedience, or make final decisions; jurisdiction. A lawful right to enforce obedience." It also means that when we are in authority, we may be appealed to for support of an opinion or act. Webster's goes further and explains the many varieties of authority: "authorizable; capable of being authorized; authorization; you have been given the authority by someone who has authority; authorized; warranted by right; supported or established by authority; derived from legal or proper authority; having power or authority."

The person who is in authority, in any given situation, generally does not have to be present to remain in authority. He can be in a different location and still command his or her authority. Depending on the leadership organization and approach, lines of demarcation can be territorial or geographical in nature.

One of the great examples regarding structure and boundaries in authority can be found in the gospel of Matthew. Jesus was teaching and healing many who were sick when a military commander approached him and asked for help for one of his servants.

> "When he had entered Capernaum, a centurion came forward to him, appealing to him, "Lord, my servant is lying paralyzed at home, suffering terribly." And he said to him, "I will come and heal him." But the centurion replied, "Lord, I am not worthy to have you come under my roof, but only say the word, and my servant will be healed. For I too am a man under authority, with soldiers under me. And I say to one, 'Go,' and he goes, and to another, 'Come,' and he comes, and to my servant, 'Do this,' and he does it." When Jesus heard this, he marveled and said to those who followed him, "Truly, I tell you, with no one in Israel have

I found such faith. I tell you, many will come from east and west and recline at the table with Abraham, Isaac, and Jacob in the kingdom of heaven, while the sons of the kingdom will be thrown into the outer darkness. In that place there will be weeping and gnashing of teeth." And to the centurion Jesus said, "Go; let it be done for you as you have believed." And the servant was healed at that very moment." (Matthew 8:5-13)

Jesus was thrilled with this Roman commander because he showed tremendous wisdom regarding authority, especially the authority of Jesus. The Roman centurion was not a Christian, or even a Jew. Like everyone other than Jews at the time, he was considered a heathen, a person who was ignorant about God. Note to self: heathen simply describes a person (who is loved by God) who has no understanding or knowledge of and is unaware of the teachings of God or chooses to deny them. He also has no beliefs in God. And since the centurion was a heathen, what could he possibly know about Jesus and the divine authority he so boldly proclaimed? Yet when he approached Jesus and His disciples, he had more understanding than most of the so-called enlightened religious people of the times. He understood and applied the principles of authority. Someone above him had the authority.

The Roman centurion understood who Jesus was and respected His authority before he even approached Him. He had heard about Jesus and the kinds of miracles He worked. He may have even witnessed a few of the miracles himself but that would be speculation. Regardless of how he knew Jesus, he had a complete and full understanding of how authority worked and knew that everybody everywhere has some level of authority over them.

He recognized that Jesus was performing amazing miracles and therefore must be reporting to someone with a tremendous amount of power and authority. As the Word says, the centurion was a man under authority; therefore, he fully understood the authority structure and how authorization or power would come down the ranks to enable supervisors at different levels to perform their duties. So when he was looking for help for his servant, he immediately went to the one who had the authority and power to help.

It's important to note that Jesus was not alone that day and the centurion had the option of going to one of the disciples. The centurion may have recognized that only Jesus was operating in the level of authority that could help his situation.

The centurion was a man in authority and under authority. He, therefore, had a great deal of respect for anyone operating in a level of power that was obviously greater than his. All military personnel are taught this respect.

In other words, "Jesus, you are obviously a great and powerful man. I am a man who has been given a certain level of authority, but nothing even close to yours. You have been given power and authority in realms that I do not understand. So please, I would not be comfortable with you bringing yourself down to my level."

The centurion recognized that all Jesus had to do was to say the word and his servant would be healed. In other words, "I know how the system works. You are in charge and whatever you say will be done."

Jesus referred to the centurion's faith as an example of how His followers were to live. The Lord desires that we understand His Kingdom principles and how those heavenly laws supersede all that we can see and touch in this earth.

> "'May the LORD, the God of your fathers, make you a thousand times as many as you are and bless you, as he has promised you! How can I bear by myself the weight and burden of you and your strife? Choose for your tribes wise, understanding, and experienced men, and I will appoint them as your heads.' And you answered me, 'The thing that you have spoken is good for us to do.' So I took the heads

of your tribes, wise and experienced men, and set them as heads over you, commanders of thousands, commanders of hundreds, commanders of fifties, commanders of tens, and officers, throughout your tribes." (Deuteronomy 1:11-15)

God establishes positions of authority and at times brings in His own person to fill that vacancy. Other times, more often than not, we elect people and place them in authority to make decisions for us and help us with our needs. The set of scriptures I just pointed out gives us an example of God developing seats of authority for the purpose of freeing his people of burdens, and men choosing the leaders to fill the vacancy.

God remains the ultimate authority. Proverbs 21:1 says, "The king's heart (which applies to leaders and all who are in authority) is a stream of water in the hand of the LORD; he turns it wherever he will." When you truly believe this and understand this principle, it will go well with you.

When Jesus was brought before the high courts, He was not shaken by what Pilate said to Him. He knew the allegations against him were lies brought on by deceitful, devious men. So he was able to stand upright with nothing to hide. He also knew God was standing in complete authority over the entire situation and was allowing these things to happen for a divine purpose.

Pilate tried to intimidate Jesus by telling Him how powerful he was and how he had the authority of life and death in his hands. Jesus remained submissive to Pilate's authority, even though He was the Son of God. But Jesus did take the opportunity to inform Pilate where his authority came from.

"Jesus answered him, "You would have no authority over me at all unless it had been given you from above." (John 19:11)

God has established authority over us for our own benefit and set a plan in place that provides organization and structure for everyone. If we were placed in the same position as Jesus and we had been given as much power and authority as He had been given, we would have probably blown up the whole town and everyone in it, washed our hands, and said, "What a bunch of ungrateful people!"

No wonder the Bible tells us to pray for those who have been given authority over us.

> "First of all, then, I urge that supplications, prayers, intercessions, and thanksgivings be made for all people, for kings and all who are in high positions, that we may lead a peaceful and quiet life, godly and dignified in every way." (1 Timothy 2:1-2)

A Lesson for the Workplace

God has afforded me many blessings during my life. He blessed me with much success as a child and as an adult. I am thankful to God for the desire He put in me to succeed and cooperate with authority. Even as a young boy, I worked well with people in charge. I minimized my questions so I could listen and understand how structures were organized and operated. I wanted to know who was in charge in order to position myself to help him meet his goals. I reasoned that if my superior met his goals and gained promotion, I would likely be invited to join in the celebration, in addition to setting myself up for a promotion as well.

Come to find out, that's pretty much how the business world works in corporate America. When a person is promoted to a new position, he needs to surround himself with a team of capable co-workers. He remembers the people who helped him most and then calls them out from the crowd—usually with a nice promotion and a little more money.

Government works this way, too. Both state and federal officials select their cabinet to help them accomplish the task of governing. One day, you are a super efficient and successful executive, working for a political candidate. The next day this leader has won the election, is on his way to Washington, D.C. and he calls you to join him.

A preacher once said to me, "You get to heaven not by what you know, but by Whom you know." I almost fell off my chair. I was so worried about my education and skills that I had forgotten the basic principle of being faithful to the One in authority over me, beginning with Jesus. I want to go along with Jesus, the One who went before me and has authority over me.

How Children Should Treat Adults

Many societies are beginning to experience the confusion and disarray that challenges civilization when the lines of authority between children and adults become obscured. Many children grow up believing they are in charge, or at least co-equal in status with their parents. Consequently, they don't have respect for authority as they become adults. I have seen so many kids struggle with self-aggrandizement and missed opportunities due to their confusion about leadership. They live in conflict until they wise up.

Rather than allowing children to believe they are co-equals in the parent-child relationship, we must teach them this wonderful promise in Ephesians.

> "Children, obey your parents in the Lord, for this is right. 'Honor your father and mother" (this is the first commandment with a promise), that it may go well with you and that you may live long in the land." (Ephesians 6:1-3)

According to Webster's, the basic definition of "obey" is to be obedient or submissive to; to comply with the commands, directions, or injunctions of those in authority; to submit to one's authority. God has established several different levels of authority over each of us.

The relationship between a parent and child is unique. This relationship is not an accident. It is God's plan from the very start. Just this thought should give each of us tremendous peace knowing that we can be blessed and uniquely bound together. Dr. David Shibley said in his book, From a Father's Heart to a Son, "Respect for parents includes an appreciation of your heritage, an acknowledging of all that has made you what you are—a unique family background mixed with both triumph and tragedy."

When children don't understand authority properly, it is reflected in the way they interact with their teachers. Several years ago I spoke with a schoolteacher. She took the time to explain many of the biggest challenges she faces. When she finds it necessary to correct a student, and then follows all of the school district's guidelines, she almost always winds up with an angry parent who sides with their child. Following the angry parent meeting, the child becomes even more belligerent.

Challenging proper authority that is placed in your child's life to help him or her can create a lifelong disadvantage for your child. You will be responsible for nurturing a warped understanding of leadership in your child's character. Unfortunately, your little loved one will have a hard time as he or she goes through life wanting to gain access into society and earn job promotions, lifelong friendships, and the necessary respect of their peers.

Respect Individuality

Choosing to love and respect each other's differences and individuality draws families closer together. It's okay to agree to disagree, respectfully. We're all unique and see life a little bit differently. We have our own preferences, and we interpret things in our own special ways. Since we were all brought up and taught to think in certain ways, we have our own subtle ways of resolving conflicts, as well as our own theories as to why things happen.

Dr. Shibley also says that "each of us place varying degrees of significance on what's really relevant and important, and we can almost always find fault with the way someone else is thinking or behaving. We can usually validate our own versions of reality by focusing on examples that, we believe, prove us to be right. The way we see life will always seem justified, logical, and correct—to ourselves. The problem is, everyone else has the same assumption."

Make Room For Authority

I love the story about the schoolteacher who kindly asked all the children in class to please have a seat. All but one sat down quickly. An obstinate boy in the back refused. So again, the teacher asked kindly and again, she met with his refusal to comply. With her arms folded she demanded that he immediately take his seat or he would be sent to the principal's office. As he reluctantly took his seat he shouted, "I may be sitting down on the outside but I'm STANDING UP ON THE INSIDE!"

This young boy was pushing his boundaries and challenging the authority that had been placed over him. No doubt, he would become a challenge for his teacher and all those who represent authority in his future unless he learns to respect authority.

Authority is not cloned from an old army movie or life experience where the drill instructor beats his troops into submission. All authority in heaven and earth is established by God. The Bible says; He is sovereign over the kingdoms of man and gives them to whomever He chooses. In other words, God raises up some and sits some down during the course of your life. The greater purpose for this is to present God's truth and wisdom for your consideration to help you make solid decisions intentionally.

All of the really major decisions in my life have been either vetted by my pastor or someone else representing authority in my life. Upon receiving my first invitation to travel and speak in India, I went to pastor Michael Hankins for counsel. He listened and committed to a time of prayer for me. When we got back together to discuss the matter, he looked at me and said, "Mark, I do not feel like this is the right time for you to go." Was that easy to hear?

I was already talking about my trip. I was very excited and so was my wife. As Kim and I prayed we had no real choice but to concur with our pastor. I chose not to go.

During the weeks that I would have been in India, my young business was faced with major theft and it left us vulnerable to vendors and creditors. At one moment during that trial, I dropped to my knees thanking God for giving me such direction through pastor Mike. If I had been absent at that time, my business could have been destroyed. Had I not made room for authority in my life, I would have faced surmounting problems.

Life Lessons

An old saying claims "blood is thicker than water." I can attest to you that this is honest and true. It is easy to forget who your family is when times are good. But when times are bad, only family will have the compassion to reach down and pull you up. I'm not talking about hitting the skids here and there. I'm talking about really tragic situations for which only family can have compassion.

> "What is desired in a man is steadfast love." (Proverbs 19:22)

> "A friend loves at all times, and a brother is born for adversity." (Proverbs 17:17)

If you choose to learn from these scriptures and the myriad others in the Bible, you will have a treasure trove to dig into during difficult and confusing times. Another truth that will help you in any situation comes from the lips of Jesus Christ.

> "And as you wish that others would do to you, do so to them" (Luke 6:31).

If you apply this Golden Rule to every area of your life, you will increase the likelihood of understanding and respecting those in authority and the family God has graced you with.

"Obey your leaders and submit to them, for they are keeping watch over your souls, as those who will have to give an account. Let them do this with joy and not with groaning, for that would be of no advantage to you." (Hebrews 13:17)

The word of God states that children are to obey their parents. Two principles apply to children who obey their parents — it will be well them, and they will have a happy and long life.

Chapter 9
Entertainment Overload

The Ritual of Amusement

The abuse of certain types of entertainment is single-handedly destroying the family unit faster than any other medium. Choosing to live your life in a manner that requires constant entertainment or activities can lead to a society that intentionally disconnects from reality rather than facing it. We can physically be in the same room with our family and friends yet, intentionally detached from those around us. The constant barrage of smart phones, tablets, computers, and televisions running in the background creates an endless stream of distraction. In effect, we become insolated from those around us and in effect, disconnected from reality.

To entertain is to divert from reality or to amuse. That does not necessarily mean entertainment is bad. Entertainment can be pleasant, especially when used in moderation. However, allowing yourself and your children to remain detached from reality through excessive distractions will produce superficial relationships at home and irresponsible adults as your children mature.

I do love to watch a good movie or football game. However, parents need to develop lasting relationships with their children. Relationships that transcend life challenges only happen when we personally interact with one another. We cannot allow a continual stream of diversion to occupy the majority of our time. As I have mentioned earlier, the years we have raising our children is limited to a very short span of time. I have visited many homes to coach families who struggle with superficial relationships and other family issues. Routinely, I recognize how these families allow bombarding distractions to replace highly necessary family relationship building opportunities. Rather than doing constructive things together and enjoying one another's company, many of these family members are isolated in personal and private preoccupations. Their home may be filled with people, but everyone is isolated in his or her own virtual world.

It's not surprising that many of these households are noticeably messy, cluttered, and dysfunctional. Is there possibly a connection here between being constantly distracted from reality and living in a cluttered messy home?

Moments and Memories

Life comes down to moments and memories. Have you ever experienced a crazy moment with your friends or family that sealed an indelible memory into your heart? These special moments are like having your own private vault filled with personal treasures that affirm you throughout life. These are the memories that build inner strength and character. When you intentionally build these memories with your children, your vault will be brimming over with joy, love and lasting smiles.

I believe one of the main reasons for the decline in family values is that children are neither taught how interact with each other nor how to be present in the moment. They are encouraged to stay distracted by television, video games or some other electronic device. Rather than being passive and allowing the distractions, have the entire family clean the house together. That may not sound like too much fun. However, when we teach children to take responsibility for the things they own, they will learn to take pride in their work and gain a new respect for their own abilities. Then reward everyone by playing a few board games, cooking your favorite meal, taking a family walk, or going out for ice cream. You must plan to spend quality family time together.

Years ago I was coaching a little league baseball team. We were tied for first place and were scheduled to face the other first place team in the playoffs. My team wanted to win so badly, but they knew the other coach had a fifteen-year winning streak as the top team in the league. So I devised a plan to help my boys overcome their intimidation. Disney had a great cartoon with a fuzzy little rabbit named Thumper! So at the next practice I let my team in on a secret. The coach's new nickname was going to be "Thumper."

I could immediately see the fear fall from their faces as the laughter began. After that, none of the boys were worried about the players they had to beat; instead their new target was to beat Thumper. When we arrived at the field for the playoff game, instead of fear and silence, our team was loose, shouting and laughing the entire time.

"Better watch out Thumper, the foxes just showed up."

"Thumper, you might want to go home now."

The crowd had no idea what my team was talking about. Even my assistant coach couldn't get over the change of heart he witnessed in the boys. We went on to win by one run and the celebration was on. I have no doubt that several of the boys have remembered that moment all these years. Many may even realize the lesson they learned. The strength that brought our team together was joy. We enjoyed preparing for the game, hoping for the victory and the release of excitement when we accomplished our team goal.

While a respect for fear is healthy, the strength to overcome these and many other challenges we will face lives deep within our hearts. So many of the fears that your children experience are directly related to the unknown. Teach your children to face the unknown with caution, excitement and confidence. The battles they win will create an inner strength and confidence from the joy that comes as they realize what they have overcome.

"For the joy of the LORD is your strength." (Nehemiah 8:10)

The Wave of the Enemy

The divorce rate in America for the first marriage is 41%. The divorce rate for second marriage is 60% and for the third marriage is 73%. [6] Clearly, the grass is not greener on the other side. Perhaps, the same habits that perpetuated the first divorce are working overtime on subsequent marriages.

From 1986 to 2000, suicide rates in the U.S. dropped from 12.5 to 10.4 suicide deaths per 100,000 people in the population. Over the next 12 years, however, the rate generally increased and by 2012 stood at 12.5 deaths per 100,000.[7] For youth between the ages of 10 and 24, suicide is the third leading cause of death.[8]

Many articles point to increased use of drugs for our youth. Daily, our children face increased terrorism, school shootings, sexual promiscuity, same sex marriage debates, cult religions, and legalized marijuana. Many children are abandoned everyday by their parents. Recent statistics estimate that we have 1.6 million[9] homeless children on our streets. "During the past three decades,

---

[6] http://www.divorcestatistics.org

[7] https://www.afsp.org/understanding-suicide/facts-and-figures

[8] http://www.cdc.gov/violenceprevention/pub/youth_suicide.html

[9] http://www.familyhomelessness.org/children.php?p=ts

the level of sexual activity in adolescents in the United States has increased."[10]

Now pause for a moment and think about this situation. Consider the alarming statistics regarding broken families, youth suicide, and increased drug use. Among teens each year there are about 3 million cases of sexually transmitted diseases (STDs), and approximately 1 million pregnancies. Human immunodeficiency virus (HIV) infection is the sixth leading cause of death among persons aged 15-24 years in the United States.[11] Can we really blame our children? Or could they be victims of a society that is more interested in participating in diversions from reality than they are in building a safe, creative and blessed home for their children?

Are parents and children alike lost in movies, television programs, video games, computers, tablets, and smart phones? Is it time to turn off the television, put down the electronic gizmos and build a safe place for our kids to help prepare them for the harsh place they find themselves in today?

Many of the habits our children build at home during the learning years may eventually become a life pattern for them as adults. If we as parents will engage in meaningful interaction with our children they will have a much greater chance of defending themselves from the peer and societal pressures they face daily.

It seems that much of our society uses entertainment and diversionary tactics like television, busyness, drinking, and many other choices to hide from problems. This typically makes our problems worse. Avoiding problems is nothing new. We all do it. We procrastinate, hoping the situation will go away. We attempt to hide from these pickles rather than work our way through them.

---

[10] Source, American Academy of Pediatrics
[11] http://aspeneducation.crchealth.com/factsheetindex/factsheetpromiscuity/

"The tendency to avoid problems and the emotional suffering inherent in them is the primary basis of all human mental illness."[12]

Spectator vs. Participator

Most of the popular entertainment available is what I will call "spectator entertainment." This type of entertainment requires practically nothing from you except your money and your emotional energy. You do not get to touch, feel, practice, participate, plan, think, help, play, run, drive, speed, jump, ski, fly, or anything else the athletes or actors may be doing. You will also most likely never develop any kind of relationship with these superstars. When spectator sports become idols, they are no longer healthy.

I am in favor of good healthy competitive sports. I also think they can provide a great family or even individual getaway. The challenge I see is that spectator sports are becoming a victim of big business. Through marketing and sales efforts, big business sports have created a multi-billion dollar enterprise with enough hype and pressure that many people feel compelled to get involved, spend money, and most importantly spend something they can never get back: their time. Time that could have been spent investing in family life and building lasting relationships.

I say this with a certain level of authority because I have held season passes to both professional football and baseball through the years. I witnessed mostly adults at all of these events. Baseball generally drew a larger crowd of children because the ticket prices were lower. The average family of four (parents and two children) will spend $150 at a baseball game for tickets and snacks. The same family of four will spend twice that at a football game. Each time I took my family to a football game, it cost $350 just for tickets and about $25 to $30 each for drinks and snacks.

---

[12] Peck, M. Scott. The Road Less Traveled: A New Psychology of Love, Traditional Values and Spiritual Growth, (New York: Simon and Schuster, 1978), pg. 16-17.

That's $500 for one outing. Obviously, these types of outings can be a real drain on a family's budget.

Sporting events can be an enjoyable family activity, but they must be done in moderation. Don't let spectator sports become an idol. If you know all the names, statistics, and records of all the players dating back to 1900, and if you know who is hot right now and who isn't, you may be a little too caught up in sports. Let's do a fact check. The next time you have a birthday, check to see who sends you a card or comes to your party. I'm sure it will not be any of these superstars who draw your attention. The next time you are sick or have a moment to celebrate, see who is with you. They deserve more of your time than the super stars do.

Note to fathers...how might your family change if you were to devote that type of attention to your spouse and children? That kind of discretionary income can be very constructive if used more responsibly. I know people right now who could write a book on one sport or another, yet many are either divorced, have children on drugs, or are unable to remember their anniversary date or their wife's birthday.

I was in my twenties during the 1970s and I watched my shared of football back then—mostly the Dallas Cowboys. I could not keep up with my dad and his interest for the game, but I did enjoy the games I watched. The famous coach of the Cowboys for over twenty years was a man named Tom Landry. Truthfully, he is the only coach whose name I ever knew. I really didn't know much about him until one night, while suffering with insomnia, I turned on my television. I saw Landry talking about the Lord Jesus Christ and offering a special book for people who needed Power for Living. It was a powerful book written by Jamie Buckingham, and I ordered it immediately. The book was incredible and God used it to change my life.

Divine Appointments

Three years later, I had the honor of sitting with Tom Landry for three hours on a flight from Dallas to Minneapolis. Ironically, I had been upgraded to first class and ended up sitting next to him. He was going to speak at a Billy Graham crusade, and I was headed somewhere on a business trip. We talked about family and the Lord but mostly about the changes in sports and the people who were coaching and playing. This was a gift and divine appointment.

Coach Landry shared his thoughts regarding the state of professional sports. "Money has changed the way we play sports, view sports, and coach sports," he said. "Sports will never be the pure competitive team-building machine it once was. The athletes are more concerned with their personal performance than their team's achievements. Money has destroyed the team-building nature of almost every major sport. Professional athletes are now more driven by their personal stats and contracts. When they change teams it is usually driven by money rather than relationships."

"How is money destroying the team concept?" I asked.

"The athletes of today are 'contract conscience' and not 'team conscience.' They will go wherever, live wherever, play for whomever, and play with whomever as long as the money is right. There is much less loyalty surfacing any longer between the coach, team, and the players." I thanked coach Landry and told him how his personal recommendation to order "Power For Living," changed my life.

In one Hollywood movie, the main character, a big-named football player, repeatedly said, "Show me the money!" It was cute and funny. I laughed too. However, we must teach our children that while earning a good living is important, our character, honesty and integrity should never be compromised to get it. When we justify our actions simply to gain the results we desire, we jeopardize our moral compass and respect for truth.

124

Somehow, big business slipped in and stole the show. In my own personal observations, I have seen a decline in the quality of people that major sports are attracting. I do not remember at any time in the recent past when professional athletes in drug rehabilitation centers were making the headlines so often. Nor can I recall a time period in which they were being arrested for possession of a controlled substance (meaning drugs) or were accused of rape, gang rape, indecency with a child, child beating, wife beating, or illegally carrying weapons in public places. I am not blaming big business for all these problems, but I do agree with Mr. Landry's assessment of the situation. Money and fame can corrupt everyone's motives if we are not guided by the inner resolve to yield to truth. Proverbs 30:9-10 NIV, the book of wisdom says:

> "Keep falsehood and lies far from me; give me neither poverty nor riches, but give me only my daily bread. Otherwise, I may have too much and disown you and say, 'Who is the LORD?' Or I may become poor and steal, and so dishonor the name of my God. "

The Bible addresses money and the issues surrounding it quite clearly. In fact, just the topic of money alone is addressed nearly one hundred and fifty times in the Word of God. 1 Timothy 6:6-10 says:

> "But godliness with contentment is great gain, for we brought nothing into the world, and we cannot take anything out of the world. But if we have food and clothing, with these we will be content. But those who desire to be rich fall into temptation, into a snare, into many senseless and harmful desires that plunge people into ruin and destruction. For the love of money is a root of all kinds of evils. It is

through this craving that some have wandered away from the faith and pierced themselves with many pangs."

The Word of God gives us clear cause-and-effect relationships for those who are geared toward gaining riches and self-glory. It clearly states that the "love of money" or seeking only after money is the root of all evil and leads to destruction. Evidence of this choice and its effects are easily seen in our society today. The next time you turn on the news or read a newspaper, look to see how much good news was reported versus how much bad news was reported and then determine how much of the bad news was related to the love of money.

My heart for the number of celebrities around the world, who have attained much fame and fortune, yet find themselves in the grips of adultery, divorce, alcohol abuse, drug abuse, and bankruptcy. Magazine headlines portray many of them living shamelessly in sexually promiscuous and deviate life styles. Someone is always swapping his or her mate for someone else. Of course, this is done legally through the courts with divorce and marriage documents. So on the surface, it appears legal, and it's what most people have come to accept.

To me however, it appears as though they live with conflicted hearts and have no real idea how to heal their inner pain and desire to be truly loved. My heart breaks for them. They are precious to the Lord and were not designed to live like this. It is simply unhealthy and unnatural.

> "Husbands, love your wives, as Christ loved the church and gave himself up for her . . . "Therefore a man shall leave his father and mother and hold fast to his wife, and the two shall become one flesh." . . . However, let each one of you love his wife as himself, and let the wife see that she respects her husband." (Ephesians 5:25, 31, 33)

Conversely, if Jesus loved the church as men of the world loved their wives, we would be in a lot of trouble. He would push us away because surely He could find a more enlightened relationship. And when He returned for His church, He would offer her divorce papers and a lawsuit asking for everything she owns. Thankfully, He doesn't operate the way we do.

Hollywood Madness

We have supported Hollywood with our time and money for over a hundred years and have helped built a giant. I'm not sure who is in charge of programming. All I know is that no one has ever contacted me and asked for my advice. The way they justify what they are doing is through rating systems and dollars. They have one goal in mind however: to get as much of our time and money as possible. They have budgets to meet and bills to pay. I realize I may sound a little cynical with my rant. However, note the amount of time you invest in the entertainment versus how much time you spend with your loved ones. We must take responsibility for the condition of the industry because our appetite for this type of programing drives their decisions.

Television only began in 1925 and movies on the big screen began in the 1890's. Yet, these two types of entertainment dominate much of our time, money, and emotions today. I can only imagine how things must have been a hundred and fifty years ago, before the first movie ran on the big screen. If all of the world's history and documentation of past civilizations, including pre-movie cultures, was lost and all we could find was fragmented archeological dishes and bowls, I wonder if science would conclude that one of the major causes of death must have been boredom—masses of people dying because they had nothing to do.

Take a look at these alarming statistics regarding our American television addiction. Then draw your own conclusions. I believe you know mine.

Television Watching Statistics

Statistic Verification	
Source: BLS American Time Use Survey, A.C. Nielsen Co.	
Date Verified: 9.7.2013	
Total Use of Television	**Data**
Average time spent watching television (U.S.)	5:11 hours
White	5:02
Black	7:12
Hispanic	4:35
Asian	3:14
Years the average person will have spent watching TV	9 years
Family Television Statistics	
Percentage of households that possess at least one television	99 %
Number of TV sets in the average U.S. household	2.24
Percentage of U.S. homes with three or more TV sets	65 %
Percentage of Americans that regularly watch television while eating dinner	67 %
Percentage of Americans who pay for cable TV	56 %
Number of videos rented daily in the U.S.	6 million
Percentage of Americans who say they watch too much TV	49 %
Child Television Statistics	
Number of minutes per week that the average child watches television	1,480
Percent of 4-6 year-olds who, when asked to choose between watching TV and spending time with their fathers, preferred television	54 %
Hours per year the average American youth spends in school	900 hours
Hours per year the average American youth watches television	1,200
Number of violent acts seen on TV by age 18	150,000
Number of 30 second TV commercials seen in a year by an average child	16,000

Television can be a source of entertainment if used properly or an enemy of communication within the family when it is abused. Today's television craze is geared around real-life events known as "reality TV." In my opinion, if it truly were reality, the show would film millions of people sitting around watching television. How much fun would that be?

How can we effectively communicate with each other when a multi-million-dollar production in 1080p HD TV is always beckoning our attention? As a father, I am concerned about the programing and it's growing need to include avant-garde ideas to express their point. They feel compelled to use a little more profanity, discuss the undiscussable, and to assault the public's concept of good taste and decency. In so doing, they are hacking away at the foundations of the family and all that represents the Christian ethic.

"In recent seasons, for example, we were offered hilariously funny episodes involving abortion, divorce, extramarital relationships, rape, and the ever-popular theme: father is an idiot. If this is "social relevance," then I am sick unto death of the messages I have been fed."[13]

Television, with its unparalleled capacity for teaching and edifying, has occasionally demonstrated the potential it carries. "'Little House on the Prairie' was for years the best program available for young children. I would not, therefore, recommend smashing the television set in despair. Rather, we must learn to control it instead of becoming its slave."[14]

The basic definition of entertainment, as mentioned earlier in this chapter, is to divert or a diversion. An insatiable diet of television and movies may divert, delay, or keep you from ever accomplishing God's will for your life. Movies and television are a valid form of entertainment, but that they can be a diversion if we are not intentional about our viewing habits.

Eyes Opened

One night, my family and I were sitting around the living room, viewing family slides. We were really having a good time, laughing about how much our clothing and hairstyles had changed. We came across some slides of Kim, when she was a child, having Thanksgiving dinner with some friends. It showed a woman— we'll call her Betty—serving the meal. Betty was the mother of one of Kim's dear Girl Scout friends, Marsha. Betty was seldom seen by anyone in her family or out in public. Fortunately, this was a spedcial holiday. She rarely even left her bedroom. She never participated in Girl Scout activities with her daughter or left the home for shopping, church, or socials. Why? As the story was told to me, Betty was addicted to television and watched one show after the other. Based on what I have been told, I believe she may have allowed the television to rob her and her family of much of the precious life God had given her.

---

[13] Dobson, Dr. James. Raising Children, (Tyndale House Publications, Inc., 1986).
[14] Ibid. PG. #.

Kim was maybe eleven years old in this picture, and even as a child she recognized Betty's TV addiction. It has remained a life-changing memory for Kim. Because of this experience, Kim would never allow herself to watch soaps or become addicted to television sitcoms and programs in any way. I know God put Kim in my life for many reasons. And one of them was to help me understand the destructive nature of television because without her help, I may have been another easy target for electronic distractions.

Betty's example may be difficult for you to comprehend. You may be doing just fine on only two hours of television per day. But remember, most of these programs feed the flesh and not the spirit. The flesh has an insatiable appetite. The more you feed it, the more it will require. Balance your time between TV, real activity and spending time with God.

You must be extremely careful with what you watch and listen to. Your eyes and ears are the gateway to your soul. What you allow into your mind will ultimately have to be stored somewhere. I have many memories created from movies and television shows that I would like to forget. They seem to lurk in the recesses of my mind and at very difficult times resurface only to create doubt, unbelief, frustration, fears, and anxiety.

> "The eye is the lamp of the body. So, if your eye is healthy, your whole body will be full of light, but if your eye is bad, your whole body will be full of darkness. If then the light in you is darkness, how great is the darkness!" (Matthew 6:22-23)

> "Turn my eyes from looking at worthless things; and give me life in your ways." (Psalm 119:37)

Another Perspective

I visited the home of Alfred Nobel, in Sweden, years ago and learned some very interesting things about this man. He was never married. He had no children, but had a large home with over thirty desks in it. Alfred Nobel was very creative and fluently spoke eight languages. Most of his education came from private tutors his entire life. But his greatest single attribute was his appetite for new ideas. When he died he held 355 patents.

His thirty or so desks were stationed throughout his home to help him with his inventions. He said he had hundreds of new ideas each month and would stop working or wake from a nap or from a deep sleep at night to write them down. No matter where he was, when the idea came, he was prepared to capture the essence of the thought on paper. As a result, Alfred Nobel's inventions made him a very wealthy man and a great contributor to the world.

We have seen many wealthy men and women come and go. But Alfred Nobel figured out a way to keep his dream of new ideas and inventions moving forward from generation to generation. He set up a trust fund that would be managed by a firm that is only allowed to spend the interest it generates. This fund generates five individual $1,000,000 prizes each year to world-changing people. Thus, the Nobel Peace Prize, as we know it, has carried on for many generations since his death.

I left his home asking myself, "Would Alfred Nobel have had the same drive and discipline he had for creativity and new inventions if he had been consumed with all the daily distractions and diversions of our time? It is quite possible that we are going to miss many of the Alfred Nobels of today because their entertainment quotas are out of balance. Instead of moments for creativity, they have to play soccer, play baseball, go to nightclubs, take dancing lessons, have tee-times at 8 a.m., watch football games, watch a movie, and whatever else we can squeeze into our already bursting at the seams schedules.

People are desperate for happiness. They will do almost anything to make themselves feel good or be happy. This is one of the reasons the entertainment industry has become so broad and so well funded. Even during economic depressions and recessions, people are willing to pay for entertainment.

Enjoyment

Movies can be a rich cultural experience that we can learn from. When watched intentionally, they can become a wonderful time of real enjoyment for a family. But we simply cannot allow this type of entertainment to become our only avenue of spending time together. Happiness is nearly always dependent on what's happening around you. And if your mood comes from external happenings, you might possibly ride an emotional roller coaster and become challenged while attempting to interact with others.

The Holy Spirit woke me from a deep sleep one night. I opened my eyes and woke my wife. "Honey," I said. "Entertainment is a counterfeit for enjoyment." Then I went back to sleep. The next day, I wrote that comment down on a piece of paper, and when I looked at the word "enjoyment," the Lord opened my eyes. For the very first time I saw the word "joy" jump out of the word "enjoyment." I could see the implications of this revelation.

> "Then he said to them, 'Go, eat of the fat, drink of the sweet, and send portions to him who has nothing prepared; for this day is holy to our Lord. Do not be grieved, for the joy of the Lord is your strength.'" (Nehemiah 8:10 NIV)

I believe God wants us to truly enjoy life. He suggests that we consider food, drink, family, and friends as a means to accomplish this. Nehemiah and his family were celebrating a sacred day. I believe that every day is sacred to the Lord and that He desires us to enjoy every day He gives us. He doesn't want us to waste our God-given time on idle conversations and empty, unrealistic fantasies heaped on us from the movie, television, radio, or music industries. Again, practice moderation for everything.

For some reason, we have grown to believe we must be doing something every second of every day. I found myself in this same trap when I was younger. It wasn't until recently that I found real enjoyment by simply being still. It is in this place that my most profound ideas come. If we do not make concerted, conscious decisions to value our time, then we can very easily find ourselves rushing from activity to activity, usually more interested in "what's next" than being present in the current moment.

Life Lessons

Children who have too many opportunities, choices, scheduled activities, and things to do are often susceptible to boredom. Our children are used to being entertained and stimulated virtually every moment of every day. They rush from activity to activity with little time in between and have schedules that look almost as full as those of their parents. If something isn't going on, they feel almost desperate to find something to do. Many kids have no idea what to do without a telephone in their hand, a television hammering in the background, an iPod wired into their ears, or a video game to entertain them.

The solution isn't to feed them ideas about what they can do to alleviate their boredom. As you know, they will often reject your ideas anyway. By offering too many suggestions about ways to keep busy, we are actually feeding the problem and supporting the notion that our kids cannot think for themselves.

Instead, when they complain about being bored, tell them it's okay to be bored once in a while. It will encourage greater creativity in your kids by forcing them to discover things to do on their own. Don't allow yourself to fall into the trap of becoming your children's activity director. Rather, teach them how to enjoy being creative using their imagination.

I believe children need to learn to be creative on their own. But I also believe that children need supervision even when they are being directed to slow down because devious little thoughts can also come to mind while they ponder the numerous choices before them.

Slow down and wait on God. Learn to hear His voice and the voice of creativity inside your spirit. By all means, learn to experience the joy in enjoyment. Limit the television as much as you can for as long as you can, and you will discover a brand-new world you never knew existed—one filled with color and beauty, majesty and holiness. Be a part of God's creation and let if fill your innermost being. You will find true inner strength from the well of the Almighty God coming alive within you. Herein lies the secret of the perfect and excellent will of God for your life.

There are three kinds of people in the world:

1 – Those who make thing happen.

2 – Those who watch things happen.

3 – Those who wonder what happened.

Let's help our children progress from number three when they are babies to number one as they mature.

"I will extol you, my God and King,

and bless your name forever and ever.

Every day I will bless you

and praise your name forever and ever.

Great is the LORD, and greatly to be praised,

and his greatness is unsearchable.

One generation shall commend your works to another,

and shall declare your mighty acts.

On the glorious splendor of your majesty,

and on your wondrous works, I will meditate.

They shall speak of the might of your awesome deeds,

and I will declare your greatness.

They shall pour forth the fame of your abundant goodness

and shall sing aloud of your righteousness.

The LORD is gracious and merciful,

slow to anger and abounding in steadfast love.

The LORD is good to all,

and his mercy is over all that he has made.

All your works shall give thanks to you, O LORD,

and all your saints shall bless you!

They shall speak of the glory of your kingdom

and tell of your power,

to make known to the children of man your mighty deeds,

and the glorious splendor of your kingdom.

Your kingdom is an everlasting kingdom,

and your dominion endures throughout all generations.

The LORD is faithful in all his words

and kind in all his works.

The LORD upholds all who are falling

and raises up all who are bowed down.

The eyes of all look to you,

and you give them their food in due season.

You open your hand;

you satisfy the desire of every living thing.

The LORD is righteous in all his ways

and kind in all his works.

The LORD is near to all who call on him,

to all who call on him in truth.

He fulfills the desire of those who fear him;

he also hears their cry and saves them.

The LORD preserves all who love him,

but all the wicked he will destroy.

My mouth will speak the praise of the LORD,

and let all flesh bless his holy name forever and ever."
(Psalm 145)

Chapter 10
Too Much Stuff

How Much Is Enough?

When I was eight years old, my family and I lived on the Military Base at Ft. Bliss in El Paso, Texas. We were extremely fortunate because the Army provided us a brand-new duplex since my father was a master sergeant at the time. We had five children in our family, so we lived on the three-bedroom side of the duplex. I remember being so excited because, even though the house had no garage, it did have a large carport in front, which provided shade like a patio cover to help block the hot desert sun in the summertime.

I have driven by the old place a few times through the years to share my childhood memories with my children and cannot believe how small the place must have been for a family of seven. Funny thing is, it never seemed small to me as a child. One time, we had guests from Belgium stay with us. Where did they sleep and how did we all fit? The memories of this period in my life, like most people's memories, are fragmented. Nevertheless, many of them warm my heart and give me balance.

As a child, I know I watched a good amount of television, but I can only remember watching a couple of programs—the coverage of President John F. Kennedy's assassination and The Wizard of Oz.

I was throwing my army green, GI Joe paratrooper into the air for one more perfect jump when my mother threw open the screen door and shouted:

"Kids, come in the house now; someone has shot the president."

As we watched the coverage unfold, it became an emotional family gathering. We cried and grieved in disbelief over the tragic loss of our president.

When The Wizard of Oz came on every year, my mother would spread a sheet in front of the television and move the coffee table. She served cold cuts and other snack food and it felt like we were having a picnic. The whole family would gather, including my dad. Mom would sit with us on the floor and Dad would stretch out on the floor with a big pillow. My siblings and I got as close to Mom and Dad as we could—looking for the perfect warm spot. The movie was a family event, not a way to keep us from boredom.

One spring, my parents invited our special friends over for a little volleyball, croquet, and Dad's famous barbecue on a Saturday afternoon. We talked about it all week. Mom had a special way of getting us all excited for special events and outings. It always included a complete house cleaning. Go figure.

As we went to bed on Friday night, we could hardly sleep because we were so excited. As an added bonus, one of our friends usually got to spend the night with us and one of us got to go home with one of the other kids. For an eight-year-old, it doesn't get any better.

Saturday morning arrived and Mom woke us early to get our chores done. Everyone jumped out of bed, bright-eyed and bushy-tailed, except for me. I didn't feel good, but I was sure of one thing—colds and the flu only happen on school days. Boy was I wrong. I was down with the flu and Mom wouldn't allow me to get out of bed. She said my fever was so bad that I was seeing things dancing around in my room.

Dad started the charcoal without me and that alone was enough to make me sick. I really enjoyed being a helper. Dad was the best at giving me projects I could accomplish with minimal supervision and still have success. But this particular day I was out of commission, and the prospect of joining in the festivities was slim.

When our friends arrived, they didn't seem as emotional over the situation as I did; in fact, they started the party without me. One at a time, they came into my room and shared their condolences then quickly abandoned me. I was banished from the festivities, or so I thought.

Shortly thereafter, my sister, Cheryl, walked into my room, and took me by the hand. "You're coming with me." She had devised a plan, with Mom's approval, to revive my aching soul. She had my dad turn the old green Pontiac station wagon around and back it into the driveway under the shady carport. She flattened out all the seats and padded the inside with blankets and a pillow, then rolled down the windows. She even provided a cooler with cold drinks, a box of crayons, and some paper. I couldn't believe my eyes.

Cheryl climbed inside first. "Come on, jump in; we're going to have a great time." She gave up her afternoon of fun, to spend it with me in the back of our station wagon. She even risked catching what I had, but she preferred me over herself, and I have never forgotten that. If that afternoon had turned out like it was originally planned, I would have played all day with my friends— maybe even had the opportunity to spend the night with one of them. But chances are I would never have remembered it as I do now, nor would I have built the lasting relationship with my sister Cheryl.

In October 1997, Cheryl lost her son, Jesse. He was a tremendous nephew and a wonderful young man with such a promising future. He loved the Lord, and the Spirit of God was radiant in his eyes and smile. He died of meningitis at a hospital in a small town in Texas. The day my sister called me from the hospital, her voice was weak. She could hardly speak and breathe at the same time.

"Mark, what am I going to do?" she said. "Jesse is dead."

The sacrifice she made for me in the back of that old station wagon flooded my memory. Lord, give me the strength to take her by the hand and walk with her. I packed my family into our car and headed in Cheryl's direction. For the next year, I called her long distance almost every day. It was my turn to just hold her hand and be there in her moment of greatest loss…her son!

One day I told her about a plan I implemented to bless Jesse in a way he would never forget. I grabbed one hundred legal size envelopes and hand addressed each one to Jesse, who was away in college. Then I placed stamps on them and stuffed each with a one-dollar bill. For the next three and a half months, I mailed one envelope every day.

When the very first envelope arrived, I received a call from Jesse. He couldn't stop laughing. We enjoyed talking about the price of postage and envelopes and the time I spent versus the amount of money in the envelope. At the time, he didn't realize I was investing in him. After the first few envelopes arrived, he caught on and began allowing them to accumulate in his mailbox before retrieving them so the money would add up enough to go to Taco Bell with his friends. Jesse never forgot that.

When I told Cheryl what I had done to bond with and bless Jesse, she was overwhelmed. She hugged and thanked me, unable to hold back her tears. We never know how long our loved ones will be with us, so we must make memories with them whenever we can. This is kind of hard to do if we are always too busy to create gestures of kindness.

How Much is Too Much?

If you were looking for a good business investment in the 1990s, you should have gone into the storage locker business. Americans buy so many things we don't need that we have to rent storage lockers to find a place for things we don't use.

I will never forget the day I stood at the door of my garage realizing why I had no place to park my car. I wished I could turn all of the stuff back into cash. What was I thinking when I bought all of it? I hope my children don't follow my example in this regard. Be careful to distinguish the difference between needs and wants.

My parents really never had much money, but somehow, we always had enough. We never did without. In fact, they bought me more toys than I needed. I have no idea where all of those toys ended up. My guess is that they bit the dust or were thrown away before one of the twenty-odd moves we made while my dad was serving in the Army.

I guess I picked up where my parents left off, buying my children toys and gadgets I always thought I wanted. The day I looked around at all of the junk we accumulated and stored in the garage, I realized my family needed to recapture the time we were losing taking care of our toys. This is when I cleared the garage, laid carpet, and made it functional for the kids. They weren't irresponsible, necessarily, but they had way too much stuff to keep up with.

I inventoried what Mark owned, knowing he was probably a typical fourteen-year-old boy who is growing up in suburban America. The list is probably much longer, but it'll suffice for the sake of the point I'm trying to make.

Personal Items List

Category: Baseball
Baseball Glove
Baseball Bat
Baseballs, Quantity -12
Baseball Caps Casual, Quantity - 5
Baseball Equipment Carrying Bag
Baseball Cleats, Quantity - 2 Pair
Baseball Uniform
Jersey
Pants
Belt
Socks
Cap
Baseball Cards
Baseball Statistics Books
Baseball Card Holder (Notebook)
Baseball Batting Glove

Category: Camping
Backpack
Handbook
Pocket Knife
Compass
Flashlight
Shovel
Rake
Hiking Boots
Boy Scout Uniform
Neckerchief
Neckerchief Slide
Class A Shirt
Belt
Pants
Green Socks

Shorts
Bolo Tie
Patches
Class B Shirt
Hat
Tent
Mess Kit
Utensils
Matches
Ground Cloth
Chuck Box
Rain Gear
Maps
Sleeping Bag
Mosquito Net
Lantern
Backpack Stove
Camping Stove
Camping Stove Fuel

Category: Shared Computer

Computer Tower
Computer Monitor
Computer Keyboard
Computer Mouse
Computer Joy Stick
Computer Software
Desk Top Publisher
Word Processor
Accounting Program
Graphics Art Program
Games, Quantity - 5
Computer Color Printer
Printer Ink Cartridges
Printer Paper

Regular Paper

Graphics Paper

Category: Other

Bicycle

Motorcycle (shared)

Basketballs, Quantity - 4

Football

Soccer Ball

Pneumatic Air Pin to Air Up Balls

Air Pump

Tennis Shoes

This list does not include school items, necessities, and clothing. Now let's expand our thought process by taking each of Mark's personal items and giving them identical value with regard to responsibility—not with regard to how often the item is used, but only with regard to responsibility for the item. The questions that come to mind are as follows:

- Who will be responsible to choose a place of storage for the item?
- Who will be responsible for keeping the item stored?
- Who will be responsible to know where the item is at all times?
- Who will be responsible to put the item away after it has been used?
- Who will repair the item if becomes damaged?
- Who will maintain the item, keeping it functional and clean?

Where Does All the Time go?

Let's drop all of this information into a time and responsibility graph. No matter how hard you squeeze, you can only get 168 hours out of any given week. That is it. You will not be able to change that unless, like Joshua, you can talk God into stopping the clock. But most likely, without God's supernatural intervention, the 168-hour allotment per week will remain constant.

Mark's weekly schedule, like most children's, will change from season to season. Depending on sports and other extracurricular activities, Mark will have to make certain adjustments to fit all of his responsibilities into his schedule. However, in a typical week during the school year, his schedule would look like this:

RESPONSIBILITY	HOURS
Sleep	56
School	45
Study	15
Meals	14
Baseball	9
Scouts	9
Church	7
Chores	8
TOTAL TIME NEEDED	**164**

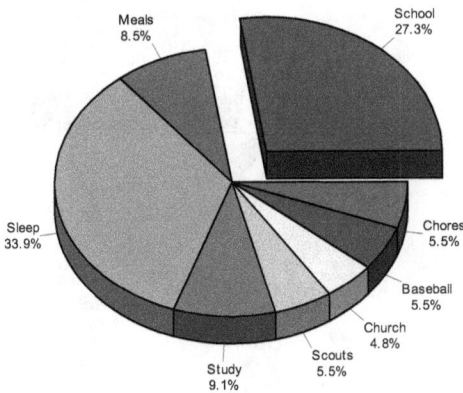

As you can see, Mark's schedule was pretty crowded. If everything in his life goes as smoothly as planned, he will have four hours per week to himself, right? Wrong. Mark has stuff and he is committed to taking care of it, and this takes time. But how much time will it take? That depends on quantity.

I put a watch to it and came up with some pretty reliable averages. In addition to using his baseball gear during a baseball game, Mark has to gather all of the pieces together three times per week, clean them after each use, and put them away. The responsibilities are the same with all of his possessions. Each time he handles an item, it requires a decision. Why am I picking this item up? What am I going to do with it? Where am I going to put it when I finish with it? These activities take time. On average, using each item for enjoyment, or just managing it, will use 1.35 minutes per day, per item.

I have only listed roughly seventy-five items. He has many more. But just what I have listed will consume around ten to twelve hours per week. You can see by this example that, like most kids, Mark does not have a spare ten to twelve hours per week. So to make everything work, something has to give.

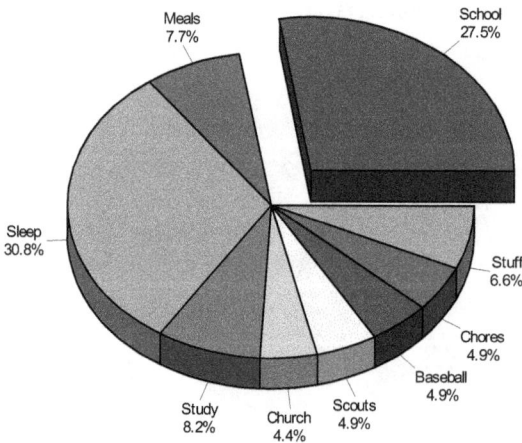

Meals 7.7%
School 27.5%
Sleep 30.8%
Stuff 6.6%
Chores 4.9%
Baseball 4.9%
Study 8.2%
Church 4.4%
Scouts 4.9%

Something is going to receive less of Mark's time and attention or he will not be able to meet all of his obligations. So the lowest item on the food chain will get lost, misplaced, left out or forgotten.

Does this make Mark an irresponsible fourteen-year-old? I don't think so. I think he has a time management problem, and probably like his mother and me, he is over-committed. The way most of us solve this dilemma is to take Mark out for his fifteenth birthday and buy him something else. We scrunch his time down just a little more. Or Mark says he wants to join this club or do this fun thing, and we let him without helping him manage his time better.

Notice that there is absolutely no time allotted for watching television or going to an occasional movie. Mark does both of these activities. I have to ask: Where does he find the time? Where is his family time? Where is his personal quiet time? Where is his help in this area? Mom? Dad? Help!

The next example shows a compounding effect. I will not change much in the graph, but I will add national averages for television and two movies per month. I will add an additional hour per day in video games, thirty minutes per day in reading, and playing outside.

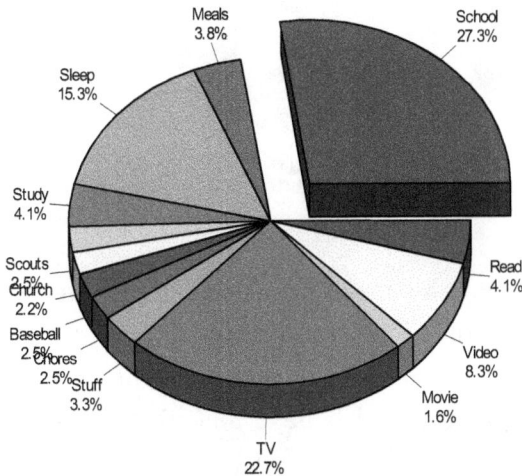

Getting pretty hard to read the different categories, isn't it? I left it intentionally hard to read to make a point. If Mark insists on keeping everything in his schedule, he will have to make some major adjustments. His sleeping time has been reduced to 3.67

hours per night. He will only be able to spend fifty-four minutes per day eating. His stuff might start lying around or get lost because he only has about forty-five minutes per day available for this commitment. It looks like he is going to have to miss a little church, scouts, and baseball because he only has about fifty-eight minutes available.

Since Kim and I are responsible parents, we will not allow Mark to reduce his sleeping or church time. I am the assistant baseball coach, so we will be at every game. I will adjust the schedule so that his time in these areas is not jeopardized. We are about to explode now. Take a look.

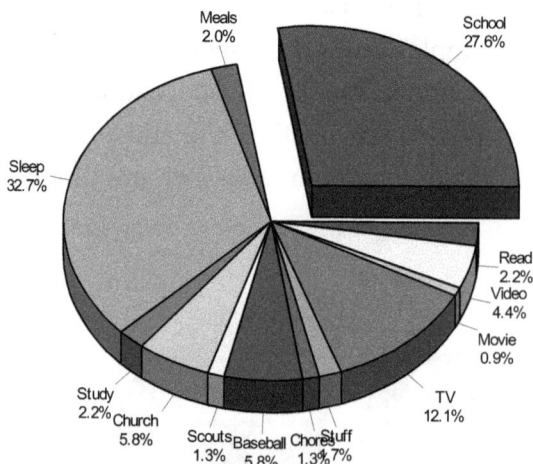

Let's slice into his mealtime, taking it down to twenty-eight minutes. We probably don't need to go any further, do we? I believe you can see a good argument against allowing our children to become over-committed. I believe that irresponsibility can and does enter into the equation, especially when the child chooses television or movies instead of taking care of his personal commitments or doing his studies. But everyone reaches a point of burnout and frustration when his life stays packed to the edges with one project after the other—one commitment after the other. Eventually, you fall prey to diversion.

We need balance. I believe that the old saying, "everything in moderation is good," has a certain amount of truth. I want to exercise caution, however. This old saying can only be accurate with respect to activities that are legal, moral, ethical, and honest.

Zondervan's NIV Study Bible includes an introduction that puts an interesting slant on the writings of King Solomon, the person most widely accepted as the author of this book. It explains that King Solomon, with his life largely behind him, takes stock of the world as he has experienced it, between the horizons of birth and death—the latter a horizon beyond which man cannot see. The world is seen as being full of enigmas, the greatest of which is man himself.

From the perspective of his own understanding, King Solomon takes measure of man, examining his capabilities. He discovers that "human wisdom," even that of a godly purpose, has limits. It cannot find out the larger purposes of God or the ultimate meaning of man's existence.

King Solomon looks at the human enterprise, he sees man in mad pursuit of one thing and then another—laboring as if he could master the world, lay bare its secrets, change its fundamental structures, break through the bounds of human limitations and master his own destiny.

He sees man vainly pursuing hopes and expectations that in reality are "meaningless, and chasing after the wind.". . . But faith teaches him that God has ordered all things according to his own purpose, and that man's role is to accept these, including his own limitations, as God's appointments.

Man, therefore, should be patient and enjoy life as God gives it. He should be prudent in everything, living carefully before God and the government and above all, fearing God and keeping His commandments. Life not centered on God is purposeless and meaningless. Without Him, nothing else can satisfy. With Him, all of life and His good gifts are to be gratefully received and used and enjoyed to the fullest. King Solomon considered his life mostly meaningless because he himself had not relied on God.15

We need to enjoy our lives and enjoy one another. We need to experience everything God has provided for us. But unless we slow down and take a hard look at each of our commitments and obligations, we may end up in our later years wondering where the years went.

I used only Mark's schedule and possessions as my model. Now imagine that time's five. Then add two adults with their commitments and things. Large families need reasonable controls.

None of Mark's schedule allowed for any real interaction with the family. He was busy every day. With that kind of schedule, will he have the precious memories I once had with my sister Cheryl? Or will his emotions, strength, and childhood get whooshed away like it never really happened?

> "And I saw that all toil and all achievement spring from one person's envy of another. This too is meaningless, a chasing after the wind. Fools fold their hands and ruin themselves. Better one handful with tranquility than two handfuls with toil and chasing after the wind. Again I saw something meaningless under the sun: There was a man all alone; he had neither son nor brother. There was no end to his toil, yet his eyes were not content with his wealth. 'For whom am I toiling,' he asked, 'and why am I depriving myself of enjoyment?' This too is meaningless—a miserable business!" (Ecclesiastes 4:4-8 NIV)

Life Lessons

If your family's schedule is overcommitted, out-of-balance or overcrowded, then you may lack organizational skills. Most likely, you simply need to learn to use a very powerful word, no! No is not necessarily a negative word nor does it make you harsh

---

[15] Ecclesiastes Introduction. The NIV Study Bible, (Zondervan Publishers, 1985)

and uncaring. It is a very responsible word that today's parents need to use more frequently. When it is used from a heart of love, your children are guarded, as they should be. This will teach them to be responsible rather than setting them up for irresponsible overloads.

When you are too rushed to keep things in order, you lose track of simple items and can spend hours in search of something as simple as a bill, a set of car keys, or hairbrushes. Take an assessment of all your family's commitments and material items. Which ones should you keep and which ones need to go? Doing this effectively will recapture much needed personal time.

Once you've created a little time or space, determine not to accept anything that will fill the newly created vacancy. Use that vacancy for family time. I'm not suggesting that you walk away from commitments leaving others hanging. Finish what you started, but then protect the vacancy.

Once your family begins to have a little free time, you will notice changes. You'll grow closer with one another, and with God.

Chapter 11
A Mother's Heart

Getting to Know Each Other

Kim was in her second year of a five-year program in occupational therapy at Texas Woman's University in Denton, Texas. I was in my third year of a five-year program in geology at the University of Texas at El Paso, nearly 700 miles away. Since email, Skype, and texting did not exist at that time, we were happy to write letters to one another daily. We could only talk on the phone occasionally because calls in the late 1970s cost twenty-five cents per minute, so we timed and coordinated our brief calls.

Sharing our thoughts and hearts in our letters really helped us to know each other. We wanted so badly to be together. By the next fall, I moved to Denton, lock, stock, and barrel (truck, dog, and guitar) because the distance had become more than we wanted to bear. Everything we did was so much more exciting, even magnified ten times over, when we did it together. Shopping to make sandwiches, going to the local county rodeo, walking in one of the rare Texas snow falls, or just sitting and waiting for our next class was all wonderful when we did it together.

By Christmas we mustered the courage to tell Kim's dad that we wanted to get married. Bob Latchaw, my father-in-law, made it pretty clear that if Kim did not finish college before she got married, he would stop paying for her education. Well, how big-a-boy was I. We invited Bob to my garage apartment in Denton, Texas. When we sat after dinner I told him that I had some good news and some bad news...which would, he prefer first? With a big laugh he said:

"Give me the good news first! It will soften the blow on the bad news."

"Ok I said, here it goes...the good news...you no longer have to pay for Kim's college tuition! It's all paid for!"

Bob rose from his chair with a loud cheer!

"How did that happen? OMG...OMG!"

"Not too fast Bob, there's still the bad news...you ready?"

"Of course, he said."

"Sit back down Bob. Kim and I are getting married next summer and you are paying for a very large wedding!"

His grand smile moved quickly from his upper cheeks to his jaw. Bob usually has plenty of snappy words to follow up any conversation. Not this time. You could see the somber in his face.

Following the initial blow, we had a great time and began to experience the joy and anticipation of the coming wedding in May. I fulfilled my commitment to finish paying for Kim's college tuition and all of her living expenses and Bob never flinched again. He pulled out the old checkbook and paid for a pretty amazing wedding with over three hundred guests.

The following May, we were married at a church in El Paso. If she had married me because I wore cowboy boots, a cowboy hat, played country music love songs on my guitar, lived near the mountain, drove a 1976 Chevy Cheyenne (four wheel drive pickup truck), wrestled at the strapping 185-pound weight class in college, and wanted to be a petroleum geologist, our marriage would have been set for a sure collapse. Most of those acquired identity characteristics weren't foundational building blocks of a successful marriage. I realized I needed to make some changes.

I changed my college major from geology to business, traded my pickup truck for an Oldsmobile Cutlass, began to dress in a suit and tie with shiny penny loafers, gained a few pounds from her awesome cooking, and sought employment in one of those downtown Dallas skyscrapers where I could leave my hammer, cowboy hat, and sack lunch at home.

We were blessed with a love for one another that was not founded on contingencies. We both knew that incidentals such as looks and the type of work we did could change in the blink of an eye, like a tragic car accident. Love cannot be based on physical attributes or abilities. It must be based on whom the person is inside.

Through our commitment to God, Kim and I have chosen to become one spiritually, physically, mentally, and emotionally. Just as we become one in Christ, God desires that we become one as a married couple. His truth solidifies our covenant and our hearts for a lasting bond together.

> "But from the beginning of creation, 'God made them male and female.' 'Therefore a man shall leave his father and mother and hold fast to his wife, and the two shall become one flesh.' So they are no longer two but one flesh. What therefore God has joined together, let not man separate." (Mark 10:6-9)

Kim pours herself into our lives. God has made her the heartbeat of our family. I believe she prefers God's will to her own and is constantly seeking the voice of the Father for continued direction for our family. She would quote Colossians 3:23-24 to us often:

155

"Whatever you do, work heartily, as for the Lord and not for men, knowing that from the Lord you will receive the inheritance as your reward. You are serving the Lord Jesus Christ."

As God gave Kim and me a desire to start a family, we decided that Kim would stop working outside of the home, once we were blessed with our first, sweet, gift from God. She knew in her heart that she wanted to be there to nourish, nurture, support, and encourage each of our children. She was more than willing to lay down her professional career as an occupational therapist to dedicate here life as a full time mom and wife. Making that decision was not the most common or popular decision in the 1980s, but we both knew it was God's will for us as a family.

Each one of our children, Mark, Kevin, Matthew, Kristin, and Kenneth, is the fruit from the seeds of this wonderful, God-given love between their mother and me. Birthing, nursing, cleaning, burping, rocking, and feeding were just the beginning. Some of Kim's favorite memories are of the times each child fell asleep in her arms after being nursed and rocked—their soft, warm breath rhythmically blowing on her skin, the feel of their silky soft hair on her neck, and the beat of their hearts against hers. And she loved to sing them lullabies, such as "Jesus Loves Me," "As the Deer Panteth for the Water," "Lord You Are More Precious than Silver," and her own melody, "Jesus, Yes I Want to Walk with You."

Looking up toward the heavens while rocking them, Kim learned that each baby had special preferences. Mark loved to have his stomach gently rubbed. Kevin loved to fall asleep as Mom drew the figure eight on his forehead. Matthew would smile himself to sleep as Mom rubbed the side of his face with the back of her fingers. Kristin's little eyes would fall shut as Mom stroked her wispy hair back from her temples. Kenneth loved to nestle his face against Mom and tangle his fingers in her hair. God uses moments like these to build early acceptance and worth into our children, and Kim valued each such moment.

Over the years, each of our children has faced challenges. Their sticker burrs, bee stings, cuts, broken arms, chicken pox, and the ever present scraped knees, have allowed Mom the blessing of giving them TLC.

As each of our children began elementary school in a classroom or in our home, she always spoke words of encouragement to them. Getting to pray over them each day has truly blessed her. She believes all that God's Word says about each of them and has been praying these scriptures over them since before birth.

> "Before I formed you in the womb I knew you, and before you were born I consecrated you; I appointed you a prophet to the nations." (Jeremiah 1:5)

> "I do not cease to give thanks for you, remembering you in my prayers, that the God of our Lord Jesus Christ, the Father of glory, may give you the Spirit of wisdom and of revelation in the knowledge of him, having the eyes of your hearts enlightened, that you may know what is the hope to which he has called you, what are the riches of his glorious inheritance in the saints, and what is the immeasurable greatness of his power toward us who believe, according to the working of his great might." (Ephesians 1:16-19)

Precious Moments

Making the children's birthdays special has been a great blessing to our family. Seeing their brightly smiling faces as we unveiled the incredible cakes Kim baked was a treat. Kim's commitment and love were manifested as she worked on special class projects in school, Vacation Bible School, Missionettes, Royal Rangers, and Boy Scout programs.

She thoroughly enjoyed helping with science projects and social studies assignments, such as making clay sphinxes from

Egypt. I can always find Kim in the crowd at baseball games. No one comes close to the amount of noise she makes as she cheers. I can also find her in the quiet place, reading one of the children a book or mending their spirits when they've had a rough time. Because of these things and many more, Kim is more special to our children and their lives than anyone else could possibly be.

A mother is unequaled on earth. God handpicks our mother, knowing exactly what each of us needs. Kim willingly and gladly accepted that calling. Because of her willingness to complete God's will, our children are here today. She reminds me of the way Mary reacted when she first learned she would carry our Savior.

> "And Mary said, "Behold, I am the servant of the Lord; let it be to me according to your word." (Luke 1:38)

Mary was a young woman, single and engaged to be married to a carpenter named Joseph—a wonderful man who was ready to love her and provide for her. Her life was already beginning to take shape.

The angel of the Lord wanted Mary to tell Joseph that God had miraculously impregnated her with the Messiah and then she was supposed to carry Him through the full term of pregnancy and give birth to Him. As his mother, she would nurture him and raise him from childhood until the Father God brought Him into His full ministry. And Joseph was supposed accept all of this. Can you imagine being in his shoes?

> "Mary looked at the angel of the Lord already 'greatly troubled' (verse 29) and said, 'And why is this granted to me that the mother of my Lord should come to me?' Then the angel explained how it would come to be and Mary, standing before the angel, probably sixteen years old or younger, said 'Behold, I am the servant of the Lord; let it be to me according to your word.'" (verse 38).

My kids are not equal to Jesus, I am not Joseph, and Kim is not Mary. However, it is still quite a commitment for a woman to decide to become pregnant, allow her body to change drastically, and then give birth to a child. Far beyond the nine months is a commitment that will last a lifetime with some eighteen-twenty years at home. If you want to put a dollar amount on it, The U.S Department of Agriculture now estimates that it will cost around $245,000 to get our children to their eighteenth birthdays. Now that is what I call a commitment. It will take both the father and the mother to pull this off God's way.

Let's continue with this trail of thought for just a bit. As an infant, each child needed to eat five or six times per day. Their mother never let them down. They soiled their diapers quite regularly and had to be changed five or six times per day. By the time they were three years old, she and I had changed their diapers and cleaned their soiled bottom somewhere around six to seven thousand times. Diapers cost about fifty cents each, so for us with five kids, that's about fifteen grand in diapers alone by their third birthday.

They would have looked quite funny going around in public in diapers only, so Mommy had to keep them dressed and their little face wiped off. She had to keep something in their mouths like food and crackers or a pacifier, just because that's what moms do.

Several years ago we had to purchase a larger vehicle to accommodate all seven family members. So we went and picked out a new van. At the same time, I was fortunate enough to acquire a new truck to get me to and from the office and around town. Our business required that I do quite a bit of driving every day.

A year later, as I was doing some preventive maintenance on our van and had to jot down the mileage, I noticed that the mileage on Kim's van was almost identical to the mileage on my truck. How could that be? I used my truck every day for work. I was constantly driving to appointments all over town. How could her van mileage match mine? The only thing she did was drive the kids to and from school and around town for a few extracurricular activities.

When I discussed it with her, I learned how wrong I had been. She was not only driving to two different schools every day, but she also took our children to various classes and meetings. Kim figured out a way to be in five places at one time. That's a commitment.

One more thing about commitment—we used a phrase around our home: "Laundry Mountain." Sometimes when I called Kim to ask what's going on, she'd reply, "I'm scaling Laundry Mountain." This was code for, "time to bail her out!" Each day, at a minimum, we had fourteen socks, seven pair of undershorts, seven shirts, a few pairs of jeans or slacks, athletic clothes, towels, and washcloths. Weekly, those numbers multiply quickly.

Many families have this same type of accumulation of laundry while both husband and wife maintain full-time jobs outside the home. I believe that is a commitment to children's lives like no one else will ever make. Just grasping a little of what your mother has committed to for you alone is worth your appreciation. You should always remember her sacrifice and she should always hold a special place in your heart. As you honor your mother and father, God will honor you.

I am not trying to create guilt for my children because of everything their mother did for them. She did it all so willingly. I just want my children to realize how committed she is to them. I also hope that my children realize that father's must treat family matters with the utmost importance.

Every woman giving birth puts her life on the line to bring children into this world. Fortunately, medical science has advanced to the point that it allows doctors to save many more children and their mothers during delivery complications than it did many years ago. Even so, The Center for Disease Control (CDC) estimates that eight hundred women in the U.S. still die each year from complications surrounding childbirth.

When Kristin was about to be born, complications set in and the doctor discussed the seriousness of the situation with Kim and me. A medical situation would mean Kim would need a C-section to save Kristin's life. Each time Kim had a contraction, Kristin took longer and longer to recover. The doctor determined that she was being strangled by the umbilical cord and she needed to come out immediately.

I was there to witness each of my children's births, and this was the second medical emergency we had out of five. As an eyewitness, I can tell you that the very last thing on Kim's mind during Kristin's life-threatening ordeal was herself. God created woman to multiply and replenish the earth. Motherhood does not exist solely to satisfy maternal instincts so they can have children to nurse and care for, but more importantly, to bring people into this world who will become a reflection of God's love for His world.

When men and women climb to the summit of dangerously high mountains and conquer feats beyond any other, we are rightfully in awe of their accomplishment. When racecar drivers exceed speeds of over two hundred miles per hour in high powered racing cars, we marvel. When astronauts blast off to outer space and live in a small compartment for weeks and even months, we shake our head. When soldiers, who are armed to kill, stand face to face in a fight to the death, it takes our breath away. When mothers subject themselves to potentially life-threatening emergency medical procedures to save the life of a baby whom they have never even met, we should be equally moved.

How Mom Helped Shape Me

As a boy I couldn't understand the value of having a great mom as I do today. Like most, with time and reflection I marvel at how moms survive untold crazy hard times and somehow maintain a deep love and appreciation for their ballistic offspring.

Rose Mary Mattingly Mullaney (how's that for Irish) was thirty when I was born. I was number four. She married my father who would was deeply imbedded in his military career. Together they had five kids and moved, lock-stock-and-barrel nearly thirty times.

Much of the time my mother was at home with us kids. But when things got hard, she saddled up her horse and headed out to help with the finances. It's not easy for a mother to leave her kids behind and maintain a balance between work, school programs, sick kids, and lean times, but she seemed to pull it off so effortlessly.

Mom had a powerful mean streak that showed it's face anytime somebody tried to take advantage of any one of her brood. She was kind, generous, and caring until one of us got hurt. Then it was time to hide. She had a way of instilling fear in the hearts of any would-be adversary. I felt safe when mom was around.

When I was barely two years old, my tricycle was stolen. The trike had a distinctive squeak that came from one of the back wheels. Mom listened for that noise when I was riding to keep track of my whereabouts. Sometime after my bike had gone missing, she heard that signature noise coming from the front of the house. Out the door she flew! The young culprit must have learned his lesson because my trike never went missing again.

How Mom Convinced Me to Pray

Bed-wetting was tolerated for a reasonable period of time. I was one of those kids who struggled with this challenge. From a kid's perspective, I'll never forget the moment that mom convinced me that I would be killed the next time it happened. Not literally, but quite effective nonetheless. She knelt beside my bed and taught me how to pray for God's help. I prayed with her that night and it worked. I awoke in the morning perfectly dry. What a victory! When I told her what had happened, her smile stretched from ear to ear. She fixed me a huge stack of pancakes. It was one of the best days of my life.

Each night following that amazing victory, I prayed the same prayer before I closed my eyes. Can't say worked one hundred percent of the time, but it was most effective and tangible. I prayed when I went camping, spent the night at friend's homes, and even when I laid down for a nap. As a result of this moment with mom, I developed a prayer habit that continues to this day. The first thing I do in the morning and the last thing I do at night is to speak with God.

No matter what life was demanding of my mom, she would turn up at every sporting event, wrestling match, court of honor, and was the first one to compliment my guitar playing while others demanded my practice remain behind closed doors. I knew when she chose my Christmas present. It was always just the right present at the right time and filled my heart with joy.

Mom always had a way of endorsing everything that I did. It gave me great respect for her and I grew from these affirmations. Even today, when she sends me a complement, I know it is truly how she feels and not some sort of hollow gesture. When she speaks truth to me, it doesn't always feel good, but if I choose to receive what she says, I find certain things in my life smoothing out.

Even though my father had some life insurance and provided a modest military retirement, mom faced entering the work place once again. She jumped in like a champion. As a professional hairdresser, she chose to build her own business from the ground up. I had no idea that my mom carried such and entrepreneurial drive. Years later she entered an entirely new career and became a million dollar producer in real estate. What a gal!

Mom chose never to remarry. But over the past forty years, she's built a business, had great success in a career, purchased several homes and managed to provide a nice retirement for herself. She and my father created a family that may run for centuries. With thirty-one grandchildren and twenty-six great grandchildren, she has to write fifty-seven birthday cards every year. She selects them with precision. Those cards are surgically precise and touch my heart at just the right time and in just the right place.

She may never fully understand how special she is to me. But I am so thankful for a loving, caring, and giving mom. She has impacted my life in profound ways. Her personal involvement in my life brings memories that flow like a river of heartwarming love.

Strength Comes From Challenges

Kim and I came from distinctly different family life styles. Her parents experienced the tragic lost of their son, Bruce Eric at age five and newborn daughter shortly after birth. One sunny summer day, the neighbors invited Kim and Bruce to go to a public swimming park that was built around a river near Parkersburg, West Virginia. Janet Rose, Kim's mother agreed that it could be a great outing for the kids.

Even with plenty of people around and lifeguards on point, Kim lost her brother Bruce that day and nearly her own life due to the river currents and depth. Nothing was ever the same at home for Kim. She not only lost her best friend and brother Bruce, but just a few months earlier, she suffered the loss of her infant sister.

No grief, can ever match the loss of a child let alone two in a matter of months. Parents should not have to bury their children. There are not words enough that can heal this kind of a broken heart. Jan and Bob never fully recovered. Their marriage ended four years after all of this tragic loss but not before the birth of fraternal twins, Bob and Bill.

Having suffered this loss and now the divorce of her parents, Kim was about to step into the unchartered waters of a broken home, single parent, and a brand new set of twins. At the tender age of eleven, she would have to step away from a desired life of both parents at home, weekends of boating and camping at the lake, and help her mom navigate turbulent waters.

Realizing her predicament and new financial burden, Jan enrolled in a computer data school and earned a diploma in data entry. She now carried the full responsibility of raising twin boys, a young daughter, and doing so by working full-time. When I first met Jan in 1978, I noticed that her heart was always troubled by not being fully available for her children. But she put on her smiley face and juggled schedules around work, violin recitals, soccer games and Kim's college activity. She did it quite well and I have always respected and loved her for her strength, tenacity, and genuine love for her children.

Kim and I were raised in two completely different worlds. I saw marriage as a solid rock; Kim saw it as vulnerable. Until my father died, I never spent a holiday without a full family, Kim spent most all of her holidays with her broken family. I saw children as someone else's responsibility. Kim saw children as her own responsibility. Our perspective was diverse to say the least.

As we married and bonded for five years prior to having our children, we recognized how our diversity could make us stronger. I learned to never take marital covenants for granted or as if they would always remain intact. Kim learned that no matter the hurdle, problems can bring couples more closely together by learning from mistakes. As I've quoted so often: "God turns all things to the good for those who love Him!" (Romans 8:28)

Life's Lessons

Raising children today may be more complicated than at any other time. When common sense is always yielded to experts and the government seems to have so much control over our children, the influence of a strong family can and will make the all the difference in their development.

My heart breaks for single parent families who are forced to make everything happen alone. I see many of the challenges that divorced couples face when they try to make time for their children and maintain a healthy environment at home. These challenges are real and will always be with us.

However, I want to emphasize the importance of nurturing, caring for, and providing stability for our children. Regardless of a parent's personal situation, a child needs to be nurtured, loved, accepted, and guided. This comes at a price. The emotional and personal costs to parents will yield great dividends as your child grows and develops inner strength and maturity.

As parents, we must accept the responsibility that comes with making the decision to have children. Children are the future of every society and they must not be marginalized. More importantly, children are living breathing human beings that deserve our personal respect, time, love, and care.

The responsibilities of a parent go way beyond simply providing a living. While that is one aspect of our responsibility, our emotional connection plays a greater role in fulfilling basic needs of our children. God will honor a parent who takes the time to nurture and raise his or her children in the way they should go.

"A wife of noble character who can find? She is worth far more than rubies. Her husband has full confidence in her and lacks nothing of value. She brings him good, not harm, all the days of her life. She selects wool and flax and works with eager hands. She is like the merchant ships, bringing her food from afar. She gets up while it is still dark; she provides food for her family and portions for her servant girls. She considers a field and buys it; out of her earnings she plants a vineyard. She sets about her work vigorously; her arms are strong for her tasks. She sees that her trading is profitable, and her lamp does not go out at night. In her hand she holds the distaff and grasps the spindle with her fingers. She opens her arms to the poor and extends her hands to the needy. When it snows, she has no fear for her household; for all of them are clothed in scarlet. She makes coverings for her bed; she is clothed in fine linen and purple. Her husband is respected at the city gate, where he takes his seat among the elders of the land. She makes linen garments and sells them, and supplies the merchants with sashes. She is clothed with strength and dignity; she can laugh at the days to come. She speaks with wisdom, and faithful instruction is on her tongue. She watches over the affairs of her household and does not eat the bread of idleness. Her children arise and call her blessed; her husband also, and he praises her: "Many women do noble things, but you surpass them all." Charm is deceptive, and beauty is fleeting; but a woman who fears the LORD is to be praised." (Proverbs 31:10-30 NIV)

Chapter 12
Sex Is Everywhere

But Not for Everyone

I regret having to discuss some of the daunting issues surrounding sexuality that our children are facing today. However, I would prefer you hear this from my perspective rather than the current stream of confusion swirling through much of our society. What I am about to address needs to be address from a father's heart.

As a caring, dedicated, hardworking father, I accepted the responsibility of talking to my boys and Kim accepted the responsibility of talking with Kristin about the truth and issues surrounding sexuality. My part of the plan included talking to the boys when they reached the age of twelve or thirteen, factoring in their individual maturity level and their social pressures.

I wanted this to be a special time—one that would block-out a firm date on the calendar. I believed it was an important enough issue that it required all of my attention and all of theirs as well. I planned a little getaway for each of my sons. Kim did the same with Kristin. I did not want this to be a forgettable passing moment. So I decided to make this an event that made each of my children feel special and a little grown up.

When the appropriate time arrived, we packed our suitcases with enough clothes for an overnighter and drove to a rather nice hotel or campground not too far from home. It was just far enough to feel like we had gone somewhere special. I took an old baby book Kim had purchased during one of her pregnancies. It was filled with family appropriate pictures, and I thought it might help make my job and the possible communication deficiencies go a little smoother.

Each of our kids was excited about going on a parent-bonding weekend, so I let them make plenty of the decisions. I will use my oldest son Mark and his trip as my example. When he turned thirteen we took our trip. Shortly after arriving at the hotel, we turned on the television, looking for the Dallas Cowboys football game, and then we called room service.

"Two large orders of hot and spicy Buffalo wings, please, and half a dozen bottles of coke, a pail of ice, and some ranch dressing on the side."

The officials blew the whistle and the game was underway. It just didn't get any better than this. You could not wipe the smile from his face, or mine as we dug into the wings and sodas. We had a terrific afternoon. We talked about everything from the football game, to baseball, scouts, school, friends, church, God, and each other. That moment will never be forgotten, however, I cannot remember who Dallas played or who won the game. My focus was not on the football game.

When the game was over, we went out to eat and see a movie. This was the first time Mark and I had ever been to a movie without the family. The movie itself didn't make near the impact I was hoping for, but it did give me a little more time to prepare for the lengthy conversation we both knew was to come.

When we returned to our hotel room, I grabbed my Bible and the baby book and pulled a couple of chairs together. As we sat facing each other, I told Mark just a little bit about what we were going to be discussing and began by letting him talk for a while. I wanted to find out what kinds of things other kids were discussing and how he was handling it.

I used the Bible to show each of my children the truth about love and relationships. I used the baby book for its illustrations and diagrams, and I dug up every bit of wisdom God had invested in me throughout the years to help prepare my children for a cruel, chilling world.

Discussing such things with my children has been one of my greatest frustrations. And it was sickening to have to reveal disgusting facts and heinous realities about the way mankind has perverted sexuality. I had to watch my children's veil of innocence fall to the ground, one by one. But it had to be done.

God had invested His wisdom in me and given me such a deep love for my children that I knew there was no one else better equipped for this task. I walked my children through the harsh realities of Sodom and Gomorrah of the Old Testament to the Sodom and Gomorrah of the world today.

I took a great deal of time to discuss the consequences of our decisions regarding sexual intimacy. I wanted my kids to know that it was not intended for recreation, but rather, for pleasure with a spouse and for bringing life into the world. I chose to teach my kids abstinence as the safest and most respectful option. God would help them if they chose to ask Him to give them strength and understanding. Puberty presents unique challenges for everyone. Helping our children understand the changes they are going through is paramount.

Each time I returned home with one of my boys, it was evident that our relationship had moved to a new level. My sons and daughter showed a remarkable level of maturity in their ability to accept the truth quietly and keep everything that had been discussed from seeping into their younger siblings' ears. This in and of itself was a blessing to Kim and me. I have always had a good, trusting relationship with my children. Each of them has confided in me for all sorts of situations. To this day, they will call me for advice when they encounter difficult issues and need to make critical decisions.

When I was a child, the subject of sex and marriage and girls and boys was summed up in one phrase: "the birds and the bees." Unfortunately, my father either never found the time to talk with me about such things or never wanted to face the delicate issues surrounding the discussion. That doesn't mean I love him any less or harbor any bitterness for his choice. But I did enter young adulthood never really knowing the truth about, or the main problems associated with, sexuality outside of marriage. Unfortunately, I ran into a few problems as a young adult, but by the grace of God, did not suffer any real serious consequences.

I do remember on one occasion while in a discussion with my older brother, mother, and father that something about sex came up in the conversation, and I was clueless. My mother looked at me and asked me if I understood what my brother was talking about, and I said no.

"Mark, I need to tell you a few things that will help you the rest of your life," she said.

For the next several days I waited anxiously, and after awhile just gave up waiting. The conversation never took place. But honestly, it really was not my mother's responsibility. I decided from my experience that I really needed for this discussion to be a priority for my children.

Sex...The Catch-all Phrase

When the word "sex" is mentioned in this day and age, most people immediately think of the physical act of intercourse or just a promiscuous relationship with someone else. The word "sex" can mean many things to many people; however, since we are trying to deal with truth, let's settle the true definition of the word.

The original definition from the American Dictionary of the English Language, Noah Webster 1828 uses the word "sex" to describe whether you are male or female. The next time you fill out a physical description questionnaire on yourself and are asked to respond to age, height, weight, and sex, you will notice that "yes" or "no" is not an option provided for your response. In other words, the question regarding sex is speaking about whether you are male or female. The questionnaire is not asking whether you have or have not had sex. That would be ridiculous. Times have changed and so have the definitions of words we use. The word "sex" has a plural meaning today.

Obviously, the magazines and billboards around the world are plastered with the word "sex," and they aren't asking whether you are male or female.

The word "sex" is used to describe all sorts of intimate contact. The word sex is so widely used that most people have become desensitized to it's actual meaning. As a result, many wrongfully believe that "casual sex" requires no commitment, no real relationship and bears no emotional, physical or spiritual consequences.

I see social markers presenting intercourse and other types of physical intimacy as socially acceptable and widely popular recreational activities. Unfortunately, sexual activity cannot be disconnected from the soul nor can it be disconnected from the consequences. God created this connection between one man and one woman for procreation and pleasure. It will always demand something deeper than the physical act.

Can you imagine the outrage or how unpopular it would be for magazines and billboards to use the truth to described what they are promoting? The headlines would read something like this: "How to Improve Adultery" or "Doctors Recommend More

Fornication." These words are considered incendiary today largely because it is hard to sweep truth under the rug.

Comes Down To Choice

Adultery, same-sex marriage and other promiscuous practices are still illegal in many states. Even so, the courts have been unsuccessful in enforcing the laws. So in a culture that no longer feels shame for wrong actions, we must make a willful choice whom we will follow. I have chosen God's word as my moral compass over the worldview. No matter what society decides to call sin, our transgressions before God do come with consequences.

> "But if serving the LORD seems undesirable to you, then choose for yourselves this day whom you will serve, whether the gods your ancestors served beyond the Euphrates, or the gods of the Amorites, in whose land you are living. But as for me and my household, we will serve the LORD." (Jeremiah 24:15 NIV).

When we change the name of our sin to more non-condemning socially acceptable nouns, we find it easier to justify wrong actions. Facing truth reveals that we all are blatantly in defiance of God and His laws. Contrary to popular belief, I am quite convinced that all people, from all walks of life, from all areas of the world, innately understand the difference between right and wrong. However, with society diluting truth through a very liberal agenda, we allow our moral compass to shift. Right becomes wrong and wrong becomes right.

> "Then the LORD God said, 'Behold, the man has become like one of us in knowing good and evil.'" (Genesis 3:22)

When God, Jesus and the Holy Spirit were having this conversation, Adam and Eve were still in the garden. It was right after God had discovered that Adam and Eve had chosen to believe the lies of the devil and ate from the tree of the knowledge of good and evil. With their eyes now opened to the truth about sin, they were sent away from the garden and out into a different world…a world that forever contends with God on just about every issue. The contention continues to this day.

Choosing to live contrary to God's design for human nature is a willful choice. It is not a biological or chemical imbalance or some sort of missing gene. Men and women are not born gay. We all have the option to make our own choice. This is the very same option for choice that Adam and Eve had when they made their decision to eat from the forbidden tree. My resolve on this issue is clear. When same sex relationships are given legal status to marry, only the law of the land has changed. God's truth, love, and laws will never change in this regard.

"Jesus Christ is the same yesterday and today and forever."(Hebrews 13:8 NIV).

"I the LORD do not change." (Malachi 3:6 NIV).

I have therefore come to the conclusion that the decision to live in unnatural relationships is an intentional decision. I also believe these precious souls wrestle with moral conflict and struggle to justify their decision. God has placed order in humanity and it is obvious that marriage is between one man and one woman. Thus, one must make a moral, mental, spiritual, and physical choice to abandon this innate truth. Every individual choosing to live this life style is innately aware that what he or she is doing is wrong.

"For since the creation of the world God's invisible qualities--his eternal power and divine nature--have been clearly seen, being understood from what has been made, so that people are without excuse." (Romans 1:20 NIV)

Society Changes - God Changes Not

One significant change I see in the world today is how society is demanding equality and acceptance of this unnatural life choice. This shift may be the result of liberal campaigns and result in civil laws changing, but realistically, God's truth will never change. I am not a hater, bigot, or a homophobe. I am simply choosing to serve the Lord and not man. I too have choices.

I love all people and do not consider myself to be a moral sheriff. I was not assigned the mission of condemning people for the choices they make. This is not the calling of the church. We must remember that we all deal with our own sin. I do my best to not point fingers at others. I simply choose to reject this life choice for me and desire that my children choose to honor God with their lives.

You might be thinking my words are pretty strong, or maybe you disagree. I am resolute and believe that God is not shocked by the choices some make. It is precisely why He chose to take all of our iniquity upon His own soul. He loves all of us and desires that we would come to know Him personally. Jesus did not come into this world to condemn it but rather to set it's captives free from the bondage of believing lies.

Sleeping is good. Sleeping is necessary. In fact, by the time you reach your eighteenth birthday you will have slept somewhere around 6,570 times. So what's wrong with just "sleeping" with him? Or what's wrong with just "sleeping" with her? I'll tell you what's wrong with it. It is a lie. You may end up sleeping, but that's not the only thing you will be doing. The truth is, you are getting together to have a sexual encounter outside of marriage. This is an example of blurring the truth with words that clearly mean something else.

Several years ago, America endured a great embarrassment and scandal at the White House in Washington, D.C. Our president at that time had been in a wrong relationship with one of his young female aids. At some point during their sexually promiscuous relationship, the young girl decided to break the news. She produced a dress that had the presidents DNA embedded in the fabric.

The president was seen on public television, eyes moving left and right of the camera and shaking his finger as if he were expressing sincere truth. The President of the United States, Bill Clinton, was recorded while making a false confession. He said; "I did not have sexual relations with that woman." We learned later that the president skirted the facts and distorted the truth. Clearly, he was playing with the words and focusing on actual definitions of the word. Nonetheless, he lied. It was the greatest scandal to ever come from the most powerful public office in the world.

Bending words does not give you a license to change truth. If you will deal honestly with the hard issues of life and stick to truth, you will have a much less difficult time resisting wrongful actions when the temptations come. We move closer to God and His purposes one good decision at a time.

God Loves All

The biblical story of the woman caught in adultery is a wonderful example of God's true concept of His love for us all. You'll recall that several legalists of the time were acting as religious cops for God, rounding up Mosaic lawbreakers. They grabbed the adulterous woman and dragged her before Christ, whom they probably saw as some kind of moral sheriff. It's worth noting that the woman was not acting alone in this affair. Obviously, there was a man equally involved. However, the man is released and never mentioned as having participated in this example of moral failure.

According to Mosaic Law, the man wasn't accused but the woman should have been stoned to death right then. Knowing this, the teachers and Pharisees asked Christ what should be done—a trick question if there ever was one. His reaction: "Let him who is without sin among you be the first to throw a stone at her" (John 8:7). Of course, no one dared move, though I would guess a few of the Pharisees wanted to. What was Christ's point? All people sin, and we don't help people who know they have done wrong by beating them up or putting them to death. When he spoke to the woman, he captured God's love succinctly: "Neither do I condemn you; go, and from now on sin no more" (John 8:11).

Sin is usually its own punishment in terms of the natural consequences it brings. To heap on top of it our own personal penalty of self-hate seems absurd and is definitely unbiblical, even though many religious groups would say the attitude is quite Christian. Yet, as one of my colleagues put it, that's like treating a sprained ankle by pounding it with a crowbar.[16]

God has always loved and even cared for all of us, regardless of the life choices we make. He personally made clothing and placed it over Adam and Eve's nakedness. His Word says His rain falls on the just and the unjust. His blessings affect all people. We as believers must remember to love all people regardless of their personal choices while standing guard over our own hearts so we do not fall into the same temptations. But by the grace of God, go I.

The real true physical excitement or sensation between a man and a woman is not some kind of feel-good, uncontrollable "animal" attraction. It is a warm and caring relationship designed by God, which requires love, affection, and commitment. The physical attraction for love, closeness, and intercourse is healthy and normal when enjoyed inside the safety and cleanliness of the godly commitments of marriage. Love requires commitments to each other, while casual sex requires nothing but a physical act that can leave you empty inside.

The Bible has a chapter which my pastor and friend of over twenty years, Pastor Michael Hankins, Church in the City, metro Dallas, calls the "love chapter." He has read this chapter to his entire congregation, from every known, accepted translation of the Bible for years. For months it appeared in in the church bulletin. It is a true snapshot of godly love for one another. I want it to be a

---

[16] Thurman, Dr. Chris. The Lies We Believe, (Thomas Nelson Publishers, 2003), pg. 143.

part of this book because I believe the heart of God glows from the words He has given the Apostle Paul.

"If I speak in the tongues of men and of angels, but have not love, I am a noisy gong or a clanging cymbal. And if I have prophetic powers, and understand all mysteries and all knowledge, and if I have all faith, so as to remove mountains, but have not love, I am nothing. If I give away all I have, and if I deliver up my body to be burned, but have not love, I gain nothing. Love is patient and kind; love does not envy or boast; it is not arrogant or rude. It does not insist on its own way; it is not irritable or resentful; it does not rejoice at wrongdoing, but rejoices with the truth. Love bears all things, believes all things, hopes all things, and endures all things. Love never ends. As for prophecies, they will pass away; as for tongues, they will cease; as for knowledge, it will pass away. For we know in part and we prophesy in part, but when the perfect comes, the partial will pass away. When I was a child, I spoke like a child, I thought like a child, I reasoned like a child. When I became a man, I gave up childish ways. For now we see in a mirror dimly, but then face to face. Now I know in part; then I shall know fully, even as I have been fully known. So now faith, hope, and love abide, these three; but the greatest of these is love." (1 Corinthians 13:1-13)

God intends for believers to walk in His love for one another, not beating each other over the head with a Bible. We are commanded by God to love the sinner (which includes all of us, I might add) and, with the fire from heaven, hate sin. This can only be accomplished when our minds are transformed by His truth. Thus, no man can boast of his personal accomplishments to sin less. When we boast of sinning less than others we are deceived and reveal our own sin of self-righteousness.

A Glimpse in the Future

The Bible speaks about the perverse generation that will be present in the end times. It says they will show up and flaunt their evil ways. It was probably no different when God decided to put a stop to it back in Noah's day.

> "But understand this, that in the last days there will come times of difficulty. For people will be lovers of self, lovers of money, proud, arrogant, abusive, disobedient to their parents, ungrateful, unholy, heartless, unappeasable, slanderous, without self-control, brutal, not loving good, treacherous, reckless, swollen with conceit, lovers of pleasure rather than lovers of God, having the appearance of godliness, but denying its power. Avoid such people." (2 Timothy 3:1-5)

With each passing day it becomes increasingly evident that society in general is "looking out for number one." For some, on a scale of one to ten, "self" would be valued at about a twelve and "others" would be valued at below a two or three. The genuine interest in helping others is still very much alive. I believe that simple things such as holding the door for a stranger, or stopping to help a stranded motorist, are fading due to the fact that so many people are so wrapped up in themselves and harbor such disrespect for others.

By simply driving down the freeway in any major city, you risk experiencing any number of hostile drivers. Driving angry has generated car wars and caused the unfortunate death of many innocent men, women and children. A new term that didn't exist just a few years ago is "road rage." The spirit that pushes the button on these kamikaze drivers is not the same spirit that the Japanese flew with during World War II to honor their country. Instead, it is partially a self-centered spirit and one of disrespect for others. The result is unfounded violence, and even death over nothing more than an improper lane change.

180

The following statistics compiled from the NHTSA and the Auto Vantage Auto Club show that aggressive driving and road rage are causing serious problems on our roads.

- 66% of traffic fatalities are caused by aggressive driving.
- 37% of aggressive driving incidents involve a firearm.
- Males under the age of nineteen are the most likely to exhibit road rage.
- Half of drivers who are on the receiving end of an aggressive behavior, such as horn honking, a rude gesture, or tailgating admit to responding with aggressive behavior themselves.
- Over a sever-year period, 218 murders and 12,610 injuries were attributed to road rage.
- One scary statistic worth noting 2% of drivers admit to trying to run an aggressor of the road.[17]

The next generation must be able to see these things for themselves and not get drawn into worldviews and trends. We must "speak the truth in love." The truth is that society as a whole is accepting practically every kind of deviate lifestyle even to the point of penalizing others who chose traditional family interests and values. God's word says this will happen. It says at some point the world will call evil good and good evil. I see it, do you?

These behaviors are in direct conflict to God and all that He is—holy, perfect, glorious, omnipotent, just, loving, kind, generous, merciful, gracious, and wonderful. He has given us guidelines not to restrict us – but rather to guard and protect us. If we as Believers allow ourselves to become involved in any type of activity that denies the deity of Jesus Christ and the Word of God as absolute truth, we deny our faith and become active participants in the antichrist spirit that is prevalent in the world today.

It is obvious what kind of life develops out of trying to get your own way all the time: repetitive, loveless, cheap sex; a stinking

---

[17] http://www.safemotorist.com/articles/road_rage.aspx

accumulation of mental and emotional garbage; frenzied and joyless grabs for happiness; trinket gods; magic-show religion; paranoid loneliness; cutthroat competition; all-consuming-yet-never-satisfied wants; a brutal temper; an impotence to love or be loved; divided homes and divided lives; small-minded and lopsided pursuits; the vicious habit of depersonalizing everyone into a rival; uncontrolled and uncontrollable addictions; ugly parodies of community. I could go on.

This isn't the first time I have warned you, you know. If you use your freedom this way, you will not inherit God's kingdom. But what happens when we live God's way? He brings gifts into our lives, much the same way that fruit appears in an orchard—things like affection for others, exuberance about life, serenity. We develop a willingness to stick with things, a sense of compassion in the heart, and a conviction that a basic holiness permeates things and people. We find ourselves involved in loyal commitments, not needing to force our way in life, able to marshal and direct our energies wisely.

"Legalism is helpless in bringing this about; it only gets in the way. Among those who belong to Christ, everything connected with getting our own way and mindlessly responding to what everyone else calls necessities is killed off for good—crucified. Since this is the kind of life we have chosen, the life of the Spirit, let us make sure that we do not just hold it as an idea in our heads or a sentiment in our hearts, but work out its implications in every detail of our lives. That means we will not compare ourselves with each other as if one of us were better and another worse. We have far more interesting things to do with our lives. Each of us is an original." (Galatians 5:19-26 MSG)

As I said earlier, the Bible tells us to test the spirits. Know whom you are talking to and whom you are spending time with. In most instances you can trust your discernment to reveal the truth about another person's motives. The primary question to ask yourself is, does this person want to fulfill his own desires and use me to fill his personal needs or is he really interested in me as a person? If you are having a difficult time determining right from wrong, then please seek godly council.

David Shibley wrote:
"You are the only person on planet Earth who can throw you out of God's will for your life. No one's words against you, no one's actions against you can throw you out of God's will for your life. No one has that kind of authority over you; only you have the power to do that."[18]

Ask God to reveal His truth and He will. Learn to test the spirits and know that God is in control. Let Him be Lord of your life.

Life Lessons

Sex and love are not synonymous. They should not be casually linked together or exchanged one for another. The word love is attached to everything from tacos to movie stars and cars to video games. Love has become a word so broadened in its use that its deeper meaning may almost be lost. Sex does not equal love and love does not equal sex.

We have explored how our society generally considers sexual acts and relationships as merely physical desires or wants being met. The emotional, spiritual, and physical ramifications are swept under the rug of "it's how I roll" rather than being seen as true causes and effects.

A father's heart of love, compassion, protection, and encouragement for his sons and daughters will create a foundation

---

[18] Shibley, David. From a Father's Heart to a Son, (New Leaf Press, 1995), PG. #.

that can keep them form looking for love or sex in all the wrong places. When our children feel truly received, accepted, and loved for who our Father God made them to be, they are much less likely to seek out or fall prey to toxic, harmful, or destructive relationships.

Chapter 13
I Love My Job (As a Dad)

Love Is Spelled T-I-M-E

My daughter, Kristin, made it abundantly clear as she sat in her highchair at the tender age of six-months that she was born with a set of lungs. While everyone in the restaurant sat calmly enjoying their meal, she would take the stage with an incredible burst of vocal prominence as she attempted to shatter all the glasses on the table. As she grew, we watched her love of song and music soar. She wrote songs in English and a few in Spanish and sang them so beautifully.

I have always considered my involvement in my children's day-to-day lives to be of extreme importance. At first, I suppose I was just curious about what they were doing and how they performed or "stacked up" next to the competition (other kids)—especially in sports, school plays, grades, music, singing, and so on. What I didn't realize, however, was how addicted and involved I would become supporting them in their own little personal endeavors. I made the decision early on to help nurture each individual personality rather than trying to shape them into any specific mold. I would take on the responsibility of teaching character, responsibility, respect, and creativity while they embraced their individual likes and dislikes. It worked.

Mark has always been a listener, learner and teacher. If he finds something that interests him, he will discipline himself to sit, listen, learn, discern, and implement. When Mark attaches himself to something, he puts his whole heart into it. We hired a pitching instructor when the boys were young. But only Mark chose to spend hour's everyday honing his baseball skills. Then used those acquired skills and made his way through college on baseball scholarships. He developed a wonder talent for story telling. He captivates his audience when he speaks. Mark finds his balance, power, and passion in truth. Don't challenge him at a game of monopoly. He resists compassion and enjoys watching his challengers squirm.

Kevin spent a great deal of time teaching himself how to use a computer. Consequently, he was the first child in our family to own a personal computer. He excelled in keeping everything he owned organized. He makes those skills look easy. When out troop went camping, his area was laid out in great detail and functioned like a well-greased machine. Other scouts, including my other sons, found their camping gear in the midst of an apparent explosion. Kevin managed to plan so well that he was generally; one-or-two steps ahead of everyone else and that gave him a clear advantage for his practical jokes. He thrives on risky but dials it down on dangerous quite naturally. His middle name should have been adventurer. At times it's hard to tell if he is serious or just pulling your chain. He loves to stir the pot, so to speak.

Matthew was a few years younger and was smaller than his older brothers. However, he didn't consider that to be a deterrent. Regardless of what his older brothers were doing, he would not be left behind or left out. So he developed a "can do" attitude that blossomed into an unmatched ability to do just about anything. If something broke, everyone in our family took it to Matthew for repair. Even today, he thrives on excelling in all he does. He loves to fly planes. I tried to show him how but destroyed the plane on it's first flight. The first time he picked up a radio remote controlled airplane, it flew flawlessly. Later in life, he began flying lessons on his own and earned the "taildragger" certification before he chose to invest in college instead. He works hard when he works so that he can get to the fun things.

Kristin is our only daughter. My parents who were from Kentucky, raised me to believe girls were special and needed their private space. It started early with Kristin. I made certain that she had an opportunity to celebrate her gender and not get swallowed up in all the overwhelming boy activity. She had her own room and her brothers treated her with respect. Her first crib had a canopy, and she always had a lot of fluffy, pink girly things. She loved being a girl. Her desires spiraled toward music, art, dancing, cooking, swimming, and emulating her mother. She's pretty good on the go-kart, loves swimming and flies down the mountain on here snowboard. She also had a risky side and pushed the envelope more times than I can remember. She was never to shy to voice an opinion. Her singing voice matured beyond it's years. When she was asked to take the lead part in a chorus, she would graciously yield the spotlight to others.

Kenneth loved to watch, listen, and learn. He was especially fond of reading. He finished reading his children's Bible twice before entering first grade. He had a personality that was completely comfortable by learning from other's mistakes. He had an acute awareness of danger and avoided high-risk situations. He was never fully persuaded by what others were doing. Ultimately, he would make his own decision, regardless of what others were doing. Maturing from the youngest into the largest of my boys, he became very competitive at 6'3 – 240 pounds in high school football. He also developed a passion to protect others, especially his family and friends. He remains that way today.

Even with the pressing demands of my career, I remained determined to stay aware of their personal needs, growth, and development. I read an article once that said love is spelled T-I-M-E. Having five children, I realized early on that for us to spend good amounts of time together, we would have to have common interests.

Bonding Activities

Camping has always been one of those common interests. From the time each child was very young, we spent many weekends under the stars, camping in some remote place. We were far from the claws of civilization—no televisions, no radios, no hot showers, plenty of mosquitoes, and yes, we were always very ready to come home. Each of my four sons earned the prestigious rank of Eagle Scout. Even my daughter thrives in the great outdoors.

Teaching them to fix things was another way I spent time with them. However, at times, I grew impatient waiting for them to figure out how to use the screwdriver or the hammer. So as soon as I could get them to surrender the tool, I would show them how Dad would do it. As I learned patience, God revealed how much more fulfilling it was to allow them to complete the task. It's more important for father's to teach than it is for them to do it themselves.

Riding bicycles was fun, but not nearly as fun as teaching them to ride. When Kristin got her first bike, she wouldn't let me remove her training wheels. After a few ice cream cones, I had her convinced that she would enjoy riding her bike "like a big girl" much more without them. Once I had successfully removed the training wheels, we took off. On her initial ride, I ran beside her until she sped up to the point that I couldn't keep up. When she got off her bike after that first ride, she gave me the biggest hug and said, "Thank you, Daddy." I was the one who felt like saying thank you. She never looked back. She rode like a champion.

Often I have purposed to do the types of activities my children wanted to do—activities such as lying in a wading pool, snowball fights, loud music, eating pizza late at night, playing hide-and-go-seek, Silly String wars, water balloon fights, laser tag, kids games, and so on. I believe we have to come down a few notches from time to time so our kids can enjoy us just like they would enjoy their friends.

God has given fathers the innate ability to bring excitement to his family. His own energy should lift the young spirits of his children to help them rise even higher than their own dreams could take them. It is so much fun watching expectations and excitement become a reality. Things that my children never thought were possible would happen and lift them to a new level of faith and an expanded vision for even greater accomplishments.

I'm Far From Perfect

I've always tried to be consistent with the way I disciplined my children, but I didn't always pull that off without a hitch. I was never inconsistent on purpose, but sometimes I was caught up in the moment. Usually, I caught myself and tried to remedy the situation as quickly as possible, but once in a while I was alerted to my inconsistency after learning I had reacted with wrong motives or actions.

Whenever I approached one of my children to apologize for not being consistent, we grew even closer because they respected me for seeing my own weaknesses, admitting them, and asking for their forgiveness.

Praying Together, Staying Together

When Kenny was just learning to talk, I used to kneel beside his bed and halfway lay beside him. I taught him the Lord's Prayer and how it was important to pray at night. Kim and I have always taken turns each night praying with our children. I loved telling the kids bedtime stories right after we prayed. Their spirits were receptive and hearts were open. They each made their own decision to become baptized.

My parents taught me an old saying that they learned years ago from a Catholic priest named Father Pank of Louisville, Kentucky: "A family that prays together, stays together." They taught me this through example from a very early age. Being involved in the spiritual growth of my children has given me a real respect and understanding of the need for prayer.

The choices Kim and I made regarding our relationship with God were no secret. We dedicated each of our children to the Lord when they were infants. We raised them in the church where they could experience truth as they were forming their thoughts and personalities. At the dinner table, we all took turns giving thanks for God's blessings in our lives.

We wanted our children to grow up realizing that prayer is a conversation with our heavenly Father, Jesus and the Holy Spirit. We wanted them to realize that they could be in a continual communing conversation with Him throughout the day.

When Matthew entered public school his teacher said that she wanted to have him go through a battery of tests. She felt he was very gifted in math and having difficulty in reading. After the results of three tests, Matthew scored extremely high in reasoning, concepts and problem solving. Yet, his verbal and reading skills were forty points lower. They wanted to give him additional help with his reading and encourage his reasoning skills.

They wanted to place "labels" on Matthew. We prayed and agreed to the help but refused them the right to label him to describe a learning challenge. We knew who Matthew was and he was none of the names they wanted to use to describe him.

The tongue has the power of life and death, and those who love it will eat its fruit. (Proverb 18:21 NIV)

We prayed daily with him, declaring that he is fearfully and wonderfully made and has the mind of Christ. He excelled through high school, did great in college and became one of the youngest licensed general contractors in California. When he was just a kid, the school district wanted to label him as slow, learning challenged, whatever! He just needed to work a little harder than the average kid in reading because in math and reasoning, he wasted the competition. Time has proven, this would have been destructive for our son. We simply wouldn't allow it! We knew otherwise. We knew the truth regarding our son. His name is Matthew. The meaning behind his name is: "Gift of God!" And that's the truth about who he is.

Here's my point. Many times Society categorizes people and declares lies over our children and us. For example, if a youth get's into trouble and winds up in juvenile detention for stealing something, will society and his parents label him as a thief? Will that take root in his life such that he considers himself a thief? These kinds of names placed on our children do not bring life to their hearts. They bring just the opposite. He may have made a mistake a few times but the fact remains, he is not a thief, his is a child of God and needs to discover his true identity in the Lord.

Saying one thing and then doing another is a recipe that breeds confusion in children. Therefore, Kim and I openly prayed before and with our children. Especially when a situation required prayer. Kim would teach the children to pray for their teachers and classmates especially if they had experienced a bad day. Praying together as a family should therefore be intentional, practical, and purposeful. Make prayer real...not religious!

Helping with Homework

This might seem like a silly topic. But I challenge you to look a little deeper. This is a wonderful opportunity to build trust and compatibility with your children. Most of their time while living with you will be spent in school. Homework is a responsibility given to them from an authority figure in their life. Perhaps by your showing interest in their homework, you show your children that it is important to follow directions and it's important to respect the wishes of those who are in authority over you.

To me, helping with homework never presented a problem. Even when I was so busy or tired from my daily work, just sitting with and teaching my children was a huge opportunity to check on their emotional strength and learning capacity. My children are each so different in practically every way. Homework however, is one of those areas where children truly appreciate the one-on-one time with dad. I could glean insight when they were struggling with certain things and help them push through victoriously.

I have always gotten a real charge out of working with my kids to help them complete their projects with excellence. When either Kim or I helped, the excitement and energy increased, and the next day when they headed out for school, they were proud to show their work to their teachers. Also, the next time they needed help on a school project, they didn't hesitate. They joyfully brought it home to Kim or me and looked forward to working together. When we did a great job together, they made me feel like a rock star.

This is such an important opportunity for parents but especially for fathers. As a dad, this shows our children that the things that matter to them are also important to us. Dad can't always be so busy that everything he has to do is so much more important than what his children have to do. Remember, their little spy cameras are running. It's always more about your actions than it is about your words.

Likes and Dislikes Are Tools

I always tried to remain sensitive to my children's feelings. I never wanted to break their spirits. I only wanted to change their incorrect attitudes and behaviors. I believe a child should have the freedom to express his or her likes and dislikes. I simply never allowed that to happen in a disrespectful or rebellious manner. I always insisted that our children, and those who visited our home, treat adults with due respect. Nothing less, and nothing more (no brown-nosing).

I could describe in complete detail the likes and dislikes of each of my children. I could also list their strengths, weaknesses, and certain fears. However, some things must remain private and never shared publically. I needed to be a confidant, not someone who would expose personal issues and secrets. Therefore, I guarded what each of my children shared and used it to help them find balance, grow in maturity, and understand how much they are accepted and loved. Not judged.

Praying for God's Calling

I have enjoyed watching as my children launched into independence and adulthood. At the time of their birth, God revealed His Spirit, which was resident in each of my children. God revealed each unique calling at different times and ages. Since then, I have been praying about these gifts but never pushing for them. From time to time, I have seen each expressing these gifts and callings. History may show that these little promises God put in my heart were realized in the lives of each of my children. I remember the story in the second chapter of Luke after Joseph and Mary had been searching three days for Jesus:

> "And when his parents saw him, they were astonished. And his mother said to him, 'Son, why have you treated us so? Behold, your father and I have been searching for you in great distress.' And he said to them, 'Why were you looking for me? Did you not know that I must be in my Father's house?'" (Luke 2:48-49)

I prayed that each of my children would know God's calling for their lives, as Jesus knew His. Kim and I always prayed that God would give us the wisdom to raise our children according His will and purpose. We never wanted to hinder God's plan in any way. As a father, the excitement of watching them grow in God's plan for their lives is so incredible, almost more than I can stand.

Gift Your Children With a Strong Work Ethic

The "w" word (work) was sometimes met by my kids with weeping and gnashing of teeth. I never intended to become a slave driver, but at times, my kids attempted to make me feel as though I was just that. I will admit, I am sort of a neat freak and I like to see things in their place. When it's time to pick up and clean up, I don't want to hear my children say, "I didn't do that," or "It's his turn," or, "It's not my week." The time and energy they expend on negotiations would almost make it easier for me to do the job myself.

However, that wouldn't help them understand the value of work and responsibility. So I made sure each child participated in appropriate work oriented projects. After they completed the tasks, they became satisfied and fulfilled. Seeing that helped me know that I took the right action. I also noticed that their personal areas stayed cleaner and organized a little longer when they knew they were responsible for maintaining them.

Life Lessons

At several times in my life I have heard people say things like, "Money is not everything." I often heard these words when I was dead broke, so these weren't heart-warming, tender bits of wisdom that I received with an open heart. In fact, my natural response usually went something like this: "Easy for him to say; he's driving a nice car, living in a nice house . . ."

I have never had a lot of money. For most of my life, I have been unable to maintain a savings account. But I have also had periods in my life in which I did have money in the bank. Money really isn't everything, but it can feel like it is sometimes.

Society often views fathers as success-driven, money-motivated people who always put business before family. For some, this may be true. But as for me and my house, this could not be further from the truth. I've worked hard and I've put in many hours toward the success of my business career and ministry calling. Since my conversion as a born-again Christian, my focus has been to free my schedule so I could be a companion to my wife and more involved as a father to my children.

I left corporate America to become an entrepreneur. I started a business without two nickels to rub together or a guaranteed paycheck at the end of the week. I believed God's Word when it says, "He will bless the works of our hands." My trust was more in God than it was in my personal skills and talents. My main motivation was always directed toward freedom—the freedom to take my wife or my children with me on a business trip. I wanted the freedom to spend time with my children during their hard earned summer vacations. I wanted my business to afford me the freedom to provide financial support for different ministries. Most importantly, I wanted to be positioned to focus on God's will and purpose for our lives.

Psalm 127 contains an incredible truth for all families everywhere:

> "Unless the LORD builds the house,
>   those who build it labor in vain.
> Unless the LORD watches over the city,
>   the watchman stays awake in vain.
> It is in vain that you rise up early
>   and go late to rest,
> eating the bread of anxious toil;
>   for he gives to his beloved sleep.
> Behold, children are a heritage from the LORD,
>   the fruit of the womb a reward.
> Like arrows in the hand of a warrior
>   are the children of one's youth.

Blessed is the man
    who fills his quiver with them!
He shall not be put to shame
    when he speaks with his enemies in the gate."

My heart's desire is to build my family, ministry, business, and personal life focused on God the Father's perfect will. I desire that He build the "house" (our lives) and not me. I prefer to give Him the glory for everything in my life. When I get to heaven someday, I want to hear not only "Well done good and faithful servant," but I want to hear that His will was accomplished through me and that somehow I didn't get in His way by doing my own thing.

Chapter 14
Reach Beyond Yourself
A final note to my kids

A Greater Purpose

It's difficult to comprehend that we are sharing a world with nearly seven billion living, breathing people. Even if we are world travelers, we will never cross paths with the vast majority of people. We have a tendency to get lost inside our own little worlds, rarely realizing how many people are in desperate need of the basics. Or, we leave it to others to meet the needs.

How many of those seven billion people have never heard the gospel? After Jesus returned from the dead, bringing honor and praise to God the Father, He handed his followers God's highest honor known to man: the Great Commission.

> "And Jesus came and said to them, 'All authority in heaven and on earth has been given to me. Go therefore and make disciples of all nations, baptizing them in the name of the Father and of the Son and of the Holy Spirit, teaching them to observe all that I have commanded you. And behold, I

am with you always, to the end of the age.'" (Matthew 28:18-20)

In plain and simple terms, we have been given all authority by the very hand of God to go into all the earth and share the gospel of Jesus Christ with every human being. Moreover, the King of Kings Himself directed us to complete this task. He gave us our marching orders and our daily responsibilities. That includes having a focus on His Kingdom work while we are alive in the earth.

As a young boy, Jesus began distinguishing himself from the crowd. He was not focused on what others were doing; rather, He was focused on what His Father had put Him in the earth to do. He was busy following the Father's calling on His life. As my children grew, I made certain they realized we all have a greater reason for being on earth at this time. In Acts 17:26-27 NIV Luke writes these words:

> "He made from one man every nation of mankind to live on all the face of the earth, having determined their appointed times and the boundaries of their habitation, that they would seek God, if perhaps they might search for Him and find Him, though He is not far from each one of us;"

We see from this scripture that God has chosen the time and place for us to reside in the earth. We also see that he arranged things so that innately we would search for Him...our Creator, Lord and God. God has a purpose and plan for everyone. But not everyone chooses to find this calling. Children can learn at a very early age that they are here by God's design. My children have understood this concept since they were very little. I have witnessed the individual passions of each of my children. Often, these passions can help lead a parent in understanding a young person's divine calling. Yet, it is beyond our reach and responsibility to place this expectation upon them.

We are to be about our Father's business. This must become an intentional focus for individuals, families, and the church regardless of denominational boundaries. Yet, we have left the commission largely undone.

Our Transition

I had been a member of the Catholic Church since birth and Kim had chosen to become a Catholic in 1977 just before our marriage. After reading the book; *Power for Living* in 1983, we began searching for a Spirit filled church and God directed us to one in Rockwall, Texas. We were living one hundred and ten miles away from this church but knew that God had placed us there so the trip was just part of the deal.

We became members right away and couldn't wait to be baptized. Then the classes started. We studied everything Church on the Rock, (COTR) had to offer. We started with the beginner classes and spent countless hours studying the bible on our own. We studied advanced discipleship and were given plenty of hands-on training.

The program at COTR included a very dynamic Sunday morning service along with bi-weekly gatherings in small groups across the Dallas, Metroplex. This paved the way for us to become connected with many other like-minded believers and to become engaged in leadership rolls. Kim and I fit right in with my guitar and leading worship together in our group. We had spent years training for this in honky-tonks and plenty of other "seedy" venues.

We made the decision to invest our time, talents, and money in the work of ministry through our local church. It was the very first time in my Christian life that I had been given the opportunity to actually participate in a work that would help so many people in so many ways.

Kim loved working with the children and I loved the opportunity to work with my boys. She jumped into the children's ministry and I began Troop 17. As the years passed, and opportunities continued to present themselves, we became home group leaders. The vision of our church was to plant four large congregations at the north, south, east, and west corridors of the Metroplex.

We inherited a small group of about twenty people from Harvey and Teresa Diamond. The group met in the Lewisville, Texas area so we traveled an hours each way bi-weekly. The new fifty-mile trip seemed close compared to our original one hundred and ten mile travel commitment. Keep in mind that our family was growing during this season. Each trip was a major move with car seats, strollers, snacks, toys, and everything else required when caring for five kids.

Over a three-year period, our home group grew from twenty to three hundred and fifty four members. Our group became so large that we had to create a directory to keep communications in order. This was part of the church plant for Church on the Rock North which eventually changed it's name to the North Church.

We enjoyed this season immensely and grew spiritually, but there was still more. Being and an entrepreneur, I knew God wanted more from me. Pastor Michael Hankins and became close friends. One afternoon while at his home, I recognized a leaking roof, mold on the walls, broken doors, and worn out carpet. In further discussions I learned that his children were suffering from continual allergies. Professionally, I was a pioneer in the Indoor Air Quality business. So I recognized several solvable problems right away.

Mike, his wife Vicki and their four children lived in a rattrap, which was provided by the church. Sigh! It was badly worn from all the other pastor's families and years of church use. I couldn't stomach the idea that we had such a dynamic church but it's pastor's were abandoned in this slum. So the first independent project God placed on my heart was to do something about their home!

Somewhere along the way I heard a profound statement and I've never forgotten it. If not now...then when? If not here...then where? If not you...then who? So I sat for days in front of my computer and designed a work spec to completely refurbish the Hankin's home.

On the Sunday morning that I proposed this makeover to our congregation, I had one hundred and twenty-five qualified volunteers line up. We had everything from air conditioning servicemen, painters, carpenters, and electricians to hospitality teams providing food, snacks, and refreshments. The church agreed to send the Hankins family on an extended vacation for about twelve days, so that was our window to complete the mission.

I scheduled the work around a twenty-four hour day, appointed supervisors to cover all the shifts, raised nearly twenty-thousand dollars, and rotated the appropriate tradesmen around each other so that they would complement each others work rather than getting in each other's way.

The project went flawlessly. There was no dissention or discord among the crews. God's spirit was present throughout the duration of the project. We completely transformed the Hankins home, with a brand new kitchen, new roof, wallpaper, plumbing, shelving, doors, irrigation, landscaping, basketball court, and carpeting. The list is remarkable. We paid for the entire project out of special donations and the church never had to tap into it's general fund resources.

On the afternoon that the Hankins returned, God gave me a vision. We cleared the home, set the lighting, turned on soft music, to give them the full impact of what God had done. No man was to take credit for this project. As we closed up the house, several of us went from room to room, prayed and anointed the doorposts with oil.

This was the beginning of my calling. It required obedience, willingness, dependence, hope, faith, love, generosity, and skill. In today's dollars we completed a one hundred thousand dollar makeover in eleven, twenty-four hour days with volunteers and our own money.

Our Lord God is so very faithful! Each time this project is brought to remembrance, His warm presence and peace touches me. I thank God for trusting me with this project.

The Night Everything Changed

I don't remember sleeping, but I certainly remember the dream. Several years past the home makeover, while lying beside my wife, I awoke from a dream that had brought me to the point of tears and crying out loud. I turned the lamp on and sat up on the edge of my bed. I had been sweating and travailing while I was supposed to be getting some rest.

In my dream I had died and gone to heaven. Jesus was standing before me with His arms stretched out. He said: "Well done good and faithful servant." I was shocked because the last thing I remembered was falling asleep next to Kim. I was alarmed because I did not feel like I was ready for heaven. I hadn't accomplished much that I could recall. As I looked across the expanse, I watched thousands of people approaching Jesus and laying crowns at his feet. The colors were magnificent and the crowns were filled with jewels.

I looked around my feet and saw nothing. Then I reached into my pockets they too were empty. I wanted to bring gifts to the Lord but I had none. Then Jesus approached me and my clothes were changed in an instant. He placed a ring on my finger and smiled.

He took me by the hand and we began to walk. He told me to relax because we were headed to the theatre of life and were going to watch a movie. Really? I asked the Lord what the movie was about? He said: "It is a movie of the life I had planned for you." You have always seemed so interested in my will for your life, I thought it might bring you a little joy."

This is when I remember wrestling with the dream. I was still in some state of sleep, but my conscience was getting involved. It's like my slumber was shorting out between my conscious thought and dreamland. I begged Jesus: "Please don't tell me that I missed your will for my life." I have prayed the Lords prayer for as long as I can remember. "Thy will be done, on earth as it is in heaven." How could I have missed it? I broke into tears and forced the air from my chest as I groaned.

As I awoke, I was undone! It took awhile for me to get a grip on what had just happened. As my breathing came back to normal and I stopped sweating, I sank to my knees...whimpering just a little. For the very first time in my life, I felt like I could speak to the Lord directly, just like I would my own father. I felt His presence as I prayed and a freedom to express everything that was knotted up in my heart.

My prayer was not very reverent nor was it as I had been trained. It was like a kid who was desperate and didn't know quite fully how to explain himself. I said: "Father, you are the creator of heaven and earth. You created everything that can and cannot be seen. You are all powerful and there is no name, no god, and no force above you. You are the great "I Am!"

Father, please hear my prayer. The desire of my heart is to do Your will. I want only to fulfill Your will in and through my life. I am submitted only to you. Since you are the creator of all, and you are indisputably the God of Abraham, Isaac, and Jacob...if I miss your will, it will be your fault. I'm all in and doing my best. I do not want to do my own thing. I am surrendered to you alone. With all my heart, I want your will and not mine!"

"I know, my God, that you test the heart and are pleased with integrity. All these things I have given willingly and with honest intent." (1 Chronicles 29:17 NIV)

Many years have passed since that night. I would most likely pray with more restraint and reverence today. However, on that night, I was frightened, young, and desperate. Even though I may have been a little disrespectful and rough around the edges, God answered my prayer with great expediency. He knew the cry of my heart was real and He knew my intent was honest.

Stepping Out of the Boat

I began taking short-term missions trips with Dr. David Shibley. He first invited me to tag along with him to India. As mentioned earlier, I passed on the first invitation. When the second invitation came, again I spoke with my pastor. This time, pastor Hankins had a peace and concurred that I should go. I got my visa, shots and passport ready.

When I arrived in India, David was waiting to fetch me from the airport. My first meeting was with missionary and ministry founder, John Gillman. In April 1968, John Gilman received a vision for spreading the gospel to the unreached, illiterate, and lost people of the world. God gave Gilman a vision to produce a movie of the gospel of Jesus Christ in third world countries with indigenous actors and local settings.

In February 1978, John resigned his position as executive producer of the Christian Broadcasting Network. He and his wife, Caroline, sold their home and risked their entire future to follow God's call and vision.

To John's surprise, when he arrived in India, the movie God had placed on his heart was showing in all the local theatres. So with great miracles, he purchased this motion picture that was filmed in India with Indian actors called Daya Saga. The response to this evangelistic tool, the movie depicting the life of Jesus, has been miraculous. India alone has over 800,000 remote villages. Less than four percent of the population is deemed to be Christian, while ninety percent are Hindu or Muslim.

Thirty-six years later, the film has been dubbed into fourteen of the sixteen major languages and has been shown to some thirteen million people in over 80,000 villages. It is estimated that 8,000,000 people have made decisions for Christ and countless baptisms as a result. These film teams, equipped with film, projection equipment, and a generator, travel throughout India by jeep, bicycle, rickshaw, and foot proclaiming the gospel. Dayspring International networks with existing churches and ministries to assure that follow up and discipleship never stops.

David took me to the London, the Dominican Republic and many stops along the way. While in India, I was asked to share on the need to give. This is a very poor nation but we had over ten thousand in attendance. I was not the main speaker so I only shared for about ten minutes. I did not call for an offering, but one began to come in anyway. Thousands began bringing everything from literally the shirts off of their backs, to sacks of rice, their shoes, and more. They brought jewelry, clothing, food, and cash. The brought their gifts for over thirty minutes.

The man hosting David's meeting was Benjamin Komanapalli. He told me that in all his years and the years working with his father, he had never seen anything like this before. He called this an historic offering! It took two pickup trucks to haul it off.

When I went down in front of the stage to pray for the sick, the crowd was so desperate for a touch from God that they crushed me against the stage. A group of men on top of the stage had to pull me up by my arms to free me from the crowd.

I could see darkness in the eyes of these precious souls. As I prayed for them I could see demons lift from their bodies and light fill their eyes. I was a Boy Scout leader/business man. This scared me so badly that I trembled. I had no idea what was going on. Yet God sustained me and His power for miracles became stronger and stronger. How could I ever return to oblivion after witnessing and experiencing the power of God freeing captives? Jesus is alive!

My last missionary journey with Dr. Shibley was to El Carmen, Nuevo Leon, Mexico. This little town of about fifteen hundred was located at the foot of a mountain about one-hour from Monterrey, Mexico.

This time, I was asked to be apart of the team teaching to hundreds of pastors. On the third day of our mission after a full morning of teaching, we left for lunch. I sat in the back seat of the car and gazed through the window at this little sleepy town. I prayed:

"Wow Lord, it would be so hard to live in a place like this!"

Then I heard the Lord's voice in my heart:

"Interesting you would say that, because I am requiring that you live here!"

"Father, I will do anything you require. However, this one time will you please do me a favor? I have four businesses with over four hundred employees, five children in school, and my wife. I have great responsibility and I cannot afford to miss hearing you correctly. My family will gladly follow me here. But, I really need to know if this is you. Would you speak to Kim for me please?

Two weeks later, Kim received a call from a couple that I had met in India. They asked her if she would come to El Carmen, Mexico and speak at a women's conference. Kim had never been out of the U.S., so this was a big deal to her. In my eyes, this was crazy!

On the third night that Kim was in Mexico, she was listening to worship music and praying alone in her hotel room. While she was praying she heard the Lord speak to her and saw a vision. He showed Kim the whole family living in Mexico and learning Spanish together. Kim shook her head and said:

"Father, I do not make decisions like this for my family. If You really desire that we move here as a family, You will need to speak to Mark." LOL

When Kim returned home, we were spending the week with my brother Charlie in San Antonio, Texas. While getting ready for the day, Kim was in the shower and I was at the sink shaving. I asked a simple question:

"Wouldn't it be hard to live in a place like that?"

Kim pulled the shower curtain back, stuck her head out of the shower and said:

"Why would you ask me that?"

We were filled with great joy and humbled when we realized that God had arranged everything. We had waited on God's word patiently for years. We had prepared ourselves by being faithful in our local church for fifteen years. Additionally, I had spent years attending seminary completing my masters in education and doctorate in theology.

I called my Senior Vice President, Lyle Mason and asked if he and his wife Brenda could meet Kim and me for coffee on the Monday morning of my return. When we sat with our coffee the first words out of my mouth were:

"It's time! Kim and I will be taking the family to Mexico to begin our journey in full-time ministry."

Lyle's only comment was:

"Well, it's about time!"

Several years earlier, Pastor Mike Hankins had a special ordination ceremony for Kim and me. Lyle and Brenda were present at that meeting. I did not know Lyle at the time. He was a Wal-Mart store director in Garland with about four hundred employees. That night during the ceremony, the Lord spoke these words to Lyle:

"You will leave Wal-Mart and go and work beside Mark in his company so that he can be released into full-time ministry."

As always, Kim and I had lunch one afternoon with Pastor Mike and Vicki Hankins. We shared with them all that had transpired and asked them to pray. Pastor Mike said:

"We have known for quite sometime that this day was coming. I was only waiting on God. Go with our blessing and know that we will always be here for you."

Baby Steps

In 1999, Kim and I left our businesses, our families, and our home. We took all five children and moved to El Carmen, Mexico to serve as missionaries. It was indeed one of the most fascinating and rewarding years as a family. I watched my children grow in their love for family and God.

We took a forward trip a few months ahead of time because we knew nothing about living in Mexico, and we had no place to live. Upon arriving, we visited the couple that I had met in India. They had a small bible school and assigned one of the students to help us find a place to live.

Felipe Neri Villarreal was his name. He chose to walk in front of the Suburban so he could pray while he searched. He literally knocked on doors and said to the occupants of the house that he was looking for place for an American missionary family to live. Towards the end of the day, he spoke with Maria Isabel Escobar. And after he had told her the story, she began to tear up and invited us to come to her home the next day.

She told us that during prayer early one morning she heard the Lord speak to her:

"Prepare your home for an American Missionary family."

She spent an entire year doing all she knew to do. She painted all the walls, tiled the floors, and built an American style kitchen with a refrigerator, gas stove and beautiful cabinets. She built four complete bathrooms in her home, which is very uncommon.

After she told us the story, we all thanked God for His amazing way of doing things. In July 1999, we showed up with a sixteen-foot tandem trailer and moved in. She and her two daughters, Marissa and Vanessa, moved into one bedroom, Kim and I had our own bedroom and all five kids shared one. Each bedroom had it's own bathroom. What a blessing.

For the first several months, Kim organized the children with home-school studies and she and I enrolled in Spanish classes at the bible school. I did a little air-conditioning repair for the school and spent time getting to know other missionaries serving in various ways.

We Witnessed Many Miracles

After finishing our family thanksgiving meal, we asked our children "how can we keep Jesus as the center of our Christmas?" My son Kevin started the conversation. He said as a family, we had always been blessed and were always on the receiving end. He simply said, "we need to be givers!" That is exactly what we did.

Kim felt like God wanted us to go the poorest areas and take the people food. Several other missionaries learned about our work and joined us. Paul and Carol Meyer had clothing. Mami and Papi Escobar prepared snacks and candy as gifts for the children. Mari, Marissa, and Vanessa Escobar provided bagged pasta for each family. Several of the bible school students joined us.

Kim and Mari loaded up the Suburban and drove to a meat plant, and picked up fifteen hundred pounds of chicken leg quarters and headed back to El Carmen. We broke all that chicken down into five hundred bags and prepared to take the food on Christmas Eve. We arrived at the Salinas Victoria, colony around ten in the morning.

Nearly fifteen hundred people live in this remote mountain village without running water or electricity. On our very first stop a young family approached our truck. One of the ten-year old girls had only shorts to wear. It was rainy and cold; we were all wearing jackets and gloves. She stood so thankful for the food. Next, Paul and Carol opened the back of their SUV and dressed her in warm clothes, shoes, a jacket and a warm beanie.

This happened all day and to sundown. We then left the colony and food to the Obrero Indians. After a few more hours we headed for El Carmen. It had been a heart warming, surreal day. In the back of the truck was a large white ice chest. We unloaded the cooler and headed off to bed.

In the morning I started to move the cooler but it was too heavy for one person. I opened the lid and counted forty bags of chicken.

"How can we have this many bags of chickens left? We handed out food for twelve hours?"

There was no way for us to have this many left. We handed out bag after bag for twelve hours. Fifteen hundred people live in that colony. We were so busy filling the need; no one kept track of the amount of food we handed out.

We believe that God miraculously multiplied the food that day and were witnesses to His mighty hand. (Today in 2014 at our church in Albuquerque, New Mexico, we have a food distribution every month. In ten years we have given away 3,000,000 pounds of food. It takes us only two hours to give out forty to sixty thousand pounds of food.)

After Christmas, every month we returned to this colony to share God's love, feed the hungry, and introduce the crowd to Jesus. Every month we witnessed God doing the very same thing. He would multiply our gift, no matter that size of the crowd, and we never came up short of food or ran out.

As a family we witnessed God's miraculous touch on many occasions. Mark was given a VIP status at the Mexican Major League Baseball Academy. He was assigned a professional pitching coach by the name of Ezequiel Cano.

One evening while preaching in Mina, Mexico, we watched a young girl receive a healing on her right arm from flesh-eating

210

bacteria. She had been treated for over a year with no success. She had to hold her arm up in the air because it stayed irritated. It was basically raw meat. In the blink of an eye, hundreds of people witnessed the healing. One moment it was red and the next it was flesh...perfectly normal.

Prayer and miracles carried us through dengue fever with Kim. Kristin contracted shingles on both sides of her neurological system and it came very close to her eye. We never got sick from the water or any of the food we ate. And drew very close as a family and to God.

We All Lived

On July 9, 2000, at 7:45 on a Sunday morning, we had just come through a mountain range in Nuevo Leon, Mexico. About two hours from the United States border our Suburban went out of control and hit a four-foot concrete pole as it headed for the center median nose first into a concrete rain culvert.

As soon as we hit the Suburban flipped end on end once and then rolled side over side six times up a twelve-foot embankment. The crash blew out all but one side window, snapped the rear axle in half and the right rear wheel broke off just before the Suburban landed in the upright position.

Kenneth, my eight-year-old son and I, had been thrown through the side windows of the vehicle. Kenneth's little body sustained many cuts on his forehead and back. Slivers of glass embedded into his forehead, lower back and spine. He was covered with glass and blood as he wept and slipped into shock. His body was thrown far from mine so Kim was divided between my location and Kenneth's.

My eye sockets continually filled with blood as the pool of blood around my head grew to over six feet. The most important thing to me before I could consider my own fate was to find out about my family. As I lay unable to move, I called out the names of each of my family members.

I began with Kim, then Kevin, Matthew, Kristin and Kenny. Mark was still in El Carmen and had no idea we had been in the wreck. With each name, I would hear their voices telling me, "I'm good", "I'm ok" and "I'm ok daddy." Kenneth could not answer so Kim assured me that he was alive and would be ok. Then she blessed me when she said that she too ok.

With that knowledge came a peace. I knew it would not be me getting us out of there. I knew only one thing to do...breathe! Keep breathing! I spent the next eight hours focusing on breathing and not falling asleep. My consciousness would come and go. At one point I have a memory of seeing everything from above.

Within the first five minutes, a man, his wife and daughter were seen running from somewhere in the desert towards us. As they arrived, the man knelt down beside me, sat a black leather bag on the ground and said to Kim;

"I am a doctor."

He opened his leather bag and began emergency procedures. His wife and daughter administered help to the rest of my family. Within the next few minutes, a bus traveling to Monterrey, Mexico stopped. About eighty people got out of the bus and cleaned up all of our personal property that had been strewn everywhere. Then, someone from the bus yelled out, "la luce, la luce de ambulancia." In English, that means, "I see lights from an ambulance and they are coming."

Within the first fifteen minutes of the wreck, I had seen a doctor and had all our personal belongings gathered and accounted for. In approximately thirty minutes, Kenneth, Kristin, Kevin, and I were carried off in an ambulance to Sabinas Hidalgo. All of this, in the middle of the desert, at 7:45 on a Sunday morning, in Mexico. We were forty-five minutes from any town and two hours from the United States of America.

The greatest of miracles was and remains the fact that we all survived with no lost no lives. Is there a God or what?

One Solitary Life

"He was born in an obscure village, the child of a peasant woman. He grew up in another village, where he worked in a carpenter shop until he was thirty. Then for three years he was an itinerant preacher. He never wrote a book. He never held an office. He never traveled more than two hundred miles from the place where he was born. He did none of the things one usually associates with greatness. He was only thirty-three when the tide of public opinion turned against him. He was turned over to his enemies and went through the mockery of a trial. He was nailed to a cross between two thieves. When he was dead, he was laid in a borrowed grave. Twenty centuries have come and gone, and today he is the central figure of the human race and leader of mankind's progress. All the armies that ever marched, all the navies that ever sailed, all the kings that ever reigned have not affected the life of man as much as that One Solitary Life – Jesus Christ of Nazareth." (Author Unknown)

As followers of our Lord and Savior Jesus Christ and messengers of His good news and serving His Kingdom while we are here in the earth, we must work together to fulfill the Lord's command, the Great Commission. We have a very definite job to complete before He will return. But it will take all of us.

> "And this Gospel of the Kingdom will be proclaimed throughout the whole world as a testimony to all nations, and then the end will come." (Matthew 24:14)

One Person

Can a single person impact the lives of present and future generations and thereby change some part of the world? I believe the answer is yes.

If life merely consists of working, eating, sleeping, recreation, entertainment, weekly to-dos, school, and a few other things, then we can fall prey to the false notion that one person cannot make a difference. I believe the average person will never impact those beyond his immediate family and friends unless he purposes in his heart to do so. If you do not stretch your heart beyond your own needs and wants, then you could miss the most important reason for which you are alive today.

Not only were we given the commission as Jesus ascended into Heaven, we were equipped and empowered to carry out His will.

"The Spirit of the Sovereign Lord is on me, because the Lord has anointed me to proclaim the good news to the poor. He has sent me to bind up the brokenhearted, to proclaim freedom for the captives and release from darkness for the prisoners." (Isaiah 61:1)

Stand Firm

"But we ought always to give thanks to God for you, brothers beloved by the Lord, because God chose you as the first fruits to be saved, through sanctification by the Spirit and belief in the truth. To this he called you through our gospel, so that you may obtain the glory of our Lord Jesus Christ. So then, brothers, stand firm and hold to the traditions that you were taught by us, either by our spoken word or by our letter. Now may our Lord Jesus Christ himself, and God our Father, who loved us and gave us eternal comfort and good hope through grace, comfort your hearts and establish them in every good work and word." (2 Thessalonians 2:13-17)

Pray for God's will in your life and in the life of your children. Stretch your heart toward others. Reach out beyond yourself. Go forth in the power of His might, and never look back.

Final Life Lesson to Strengthen You

Of course, I would have to close with a movie line by one of my favorites... Sylvester Stallone as Rocky Balboa from his movie "Balboa"...

"Let me tell you something you already know. The world ain't all sunshine and rainbows. It's a very mean and nasty place. And I don't care how tough you are. It will beat you to your knees and keep you permanently there if you let it. You, me, or nobody is gonna hit as hard as life, but it ain't about how hard you hit, it's about how hard you can get hit and keep moving forward, how much you can take and keep moving forward. That's how winning is done. Now if you know what you are worth, go out and get what you are worth, but you gotta be willing to take the hits and not pointing fingers, saying you ain't where you want to be because of him or her or anybody. Cowards do that, and that ain't you. You're better than that!"[19] –Rocky Balboa

To all of my children, grandchildren, family to come, and anyone else gleaning from my thoughts, please think about the deeper things mentioned in this quote. I chose this to close my book because it is so real and down to earth. You must not allow the hard times in your life or the negative people around you to define you. Rather, use the hard times to strengthen your resolve and learn from them. Remember that the negative things said about you only reveal the heart condition from which they came. Let your inner passions, purpose and God define who you are, where you go, and how you get there. Stay true to yourself and above all, stay true to God, Jesus, and the Holy Spirit.

---

[19] www.imdb.com/title/tt0479143/quotes

BIBLIOGRAPHY

Carlson, Richard, Ph.D., Don't Sweat The Small Stuff with Your Family, Hyperion, 1998.

Damazio, Frank, The Making of a Leader, Bible Temple Publishing, 1988.

Dobson, Dr. James, Raising Children, Tyndale House Publishers, Inc., 1982.

"Ecclesiastes Introduction," The NIV Study Bible, Zondervan Bible Publishers, 1985.

Gilman, John, They're Killing an Innocent Man, Dayspring International, Inc., 1998.

Lockyer R.S.L., Dr. Herbert, All The Women of The Bible, Zondervan Books, 1988.

McDowell, Josh & Wakefield, Dr. Norman, The Dad Difference, Here's Life Publishers, 1989.

Peck, M. Scott, The Road Less Traveled: A New Psychology of Love, Traditional Values and Spiritual Growth, Simon and Schuster, 1978.

Shibley, David, Heaven's Heroes, New Leaf Press, 1989, 1993.

Shibley, David, From a Father's Heart to a Son, New Leaf Press, 1995.

Smalley, Gary & Trent Ph.D, John, Leaving The Light On, Multnomah Books, 1994.

The Open Bible Expanded Edition, New American Standard, Thomas Nelson Publishers, 1985.

Thurman, Dr. Chris, The Lies We Believe, Thomas Nelson Publishers, Nashville, 1989.

www.ingramcontent.com/pod-product-compliance
Lightning Source LLC
Chambersburg PA
CBHW061143040426
42445CB00013B/1522